GW00372748

To be a Pilot

To be a Pilot

Mike Jerram

Airlife
England

This third edition published in the UK in 1991 by Airlife Publishing Ltd.
First edition published 1982, second edition 1988.

British Library Cataloguing in Publication Data
    Jerram, Michael F. *1945–*
    To be a pilot. –3rd. ed.
    1. Flying (Aircraft)
    I. Title
    629.13252023

    ISBN 1 85310 262 8

Printed by Livesey Ltd, Shrewsbury

Airlife Publishing Ltd.
101 Longden Road, Shrewsbury, England

Contents

"A flying career is much more than just a meal-ticket with fringe benefits. You will find an endless fascination in all aeronautical matters, you will find that you are constantly being challenged by new equipment, new techniques, new concepts. You will find that you have got to keep on top of a flying job both for your own peace of mind as well as for the safety of the people who put themselves in your care."

HRH The Duke of Edinburgh.

Preface

Don't envy the birds, join them! If you can drive a car, you can fly an aeroplane!
So claim encouraging advertisements from light aircraft manufacturers and flying schools. You have probably seen them, and perhaps wondered if it can possibly be true. Can anyone learn to fly? Could you do it?

The answer is a qualified Yes. Just about anyone could be taught to handle the controls of an aeroplane without instant disaster befalling them. Young children have done it. So have elderly grandmothers (though not necessarily from the same family. . .). But in truth the most commonly quoted parallel — between driving and flying — is not really a valid comparison. Flying an aeroplane can actually be easier than driving a car. There is much less traffic to worry about, for one thing. But flying does demand quite different skills, and levels of skill, to those required of the motorist. A pilot needs co-ordination of mind, hand and eye which quite simply is not an inherent part of everyone's make-up. Just as a few people are 'natural' drivers or sports players, so many struggle to master even the basic rudiments, and some never do.

To oversimplify: a pilot needs a good driver's co-ordination and reflexes; a horserider's sense of balance and subtle touch of hand; a sailor's eye for weather, and much else besides. Yes, it is possible to teach almost anyone the basic mechanical ability to control an aeroplane in flight, but not everyone is capable of honing that skill to the level necessary to become a safe and proficient pilot.

This is not intended to be a textbook for those wishing to learn how to fly. There are many excellent training manuals on the market which deal with the subject in more exhaustive detail and with greater authority than would be possible or desirable in the context of this book, whose purpose is to whet the appetites of aspiring private and professional fliers and, I hope, to help answer that question: Could I do it? Could I fly? Do I have what it takes TO BE A PILOT?

Acknowledgements

For their help in supplying information for the first and second editions of *To be a Pilot* and for this revised edition, the author would like to thank: Air Commodore C. A. Alldis, CBE, DFC, AFC, MA, Secretary to The Air League Educational Trust; the British Airline Pilots' Association; Captain Graham Jenkins, former Manager of Flight Crew Resourcing at British Airways; the Flight Crew Licensing and Information and Publicity departments of the Civil Aviation Authority; Danny Forman, MBE, Chief Executive of the General Aviation Manufacturers & Traders Association; Miss Hazel Prosper, Corps Director of the Girls Venture Corps; Jack Nicholl, Peter Latham and Colin Beckwith, past Principals of Oxford Air Training School; James Gilbert, Editor of *Pilot*, for permission to adapt certain material which first appeared in that magazine; Flight Lieutenant Larry Chamberlain of HQ Air Cadets, RAF Newton; Squadron Leader G. L. Margitta. BA, RAF, Royal Air Force College Cranwell; the staffs of the Army, Royal Air Force and Royal Navy Careers Offices; the public relations staff of British Airways, British Aerospace, RAF Strike and Support Commands; and those many students, pilots, instructors and others whose brains I have picked over the years.

Mike Jerram
Lincolnshire
September 1990

Chapter 1
About Aeroplanes

Whatever your eventual aim in aviation, be it simply a desire to fly for recreation as a private pilot, to become an airline pilot, or a fighter pilot, your basic tool will be the same: an aeroplane. And since every would-be flier's first introduction to flying is likely to be in a small training aeroplane, you may find the major part of this book, which is devoted to the particulars of becoming a pilot, easier to follow if we take time first to cast an eye over a typical modern light aeroplane of the kind used for instructing trainee pilots.

Most flying schools in Britain use either American or French aircraft, although new British light aircraft such as the Slingsby T67 Firefly are also in widespread use. But the types most likely to be encountered at any typical flying school are still the American-designed high-wing Cessna 150, 152 and Aerobat and the low-wing Piper Tomahawk, Cherokee, Cadet and Warrior, Gulfstream Cheetah and Tiger, and French Robins. All are similar in concept: two or four-seaters with side-by-side seating, fixed tricycle undercarriages — that is with a nosewheel at the front — and four-cylinder horizontally-opposed piston engines in the 100-180 horsepower range. There are flying schools which operate tailwheel aircraft for training, and should you wish, it is still possible to learn to fly in vintage open-cockpit aeroplanes such as the Tiger Moth, which first began training neophyte pilots over half a century ago.

Let us look at one of the most common training aeroplanes: a Cessna 152. The high wing configuration is not everyone's favourite, because the wings limit the pilot's vision overhead and when the aircraft is turning, but in a

1

downward direction visibility is generally quite good. Conversely, in a low-wing type such as the Cadet, upward visibility is less restricted but the wings obscure a substantial part of the downward view. Aircraft with large clear canopies such as the Robin 200 and 400 series and the Slingsby T67 provide the best compromise, but it is still a case of swings and roundabouts. Each configuration has its champions. In common with all conventional aircraft the Cessna 152's airframe comprises three primary elements: the fuselage, which contains the cockpit or cabin area; an engine, in this case a 108 horsepower Textron-Lycoming O-235 mounted at the front of the fuselage; and flying surfaces — wings and tail group. These in turn have movable control surfaces which, when used in various combinations, direct the movement of the aircraft in the air.

Let us look first at the tail group. The horizontal surface is known as the tailplane or, in American parlance, the stabiliser. Its hinged rear portions are known as elevators. Some aircraft have tailplanes which move in their entirety, and are popularly called 'stabilators'. Elevators control the aircraft in the pitch axis. Imagine the aircraft in side (profile) view. Its centre of gravity is roughly at a point one quarter to one third back from the forward (leading) edge of the wing. Now imagine an axis or shaft passing through that point from wingtip to wingtip. In pitch the aircraft will pivot about that axis, nose up or nose down, and the hinged elevators control the direction of that movement. By raising the elevators using the control wheel or stick (more about those later) a downward force is created on the aircraft's tail in flight, thus raising the nose, and vice-versa. Inset into one elevator is a smaller hinged surface. It is called a trim tab, and its function is to relieve the pilot of the control force needed to hold the elevators at any desired angle, to trim the aeroplane at a selected pitch angle. It is moved by a small wheel in the cockpit and the tab moves in the opposite direction to the desired elevator movement: trim tab down, elevator up; trim tab up, elevator down.

The fixed vertical tail surface is called a fin. Its rakish angle of sweepback is more for reasons of styling than for aerodynamic purposes. The hinged rear surface of the fin is the rudder. Its function is to control the aeroplane in its yaw axis. Let us return to our centre of gravity spot, but this time imagine the aircraft in plan view as if seen from directly above, with the axis or shaft passing vertically through its centre of gravity. Now imagine the nose of the aeroplane swinging round from side to side as it revolves around the axis. That is yaw, and it is controlled by the rudder, which is operated by a pair of rudder (foot) pedals.

Let us look now at the Cessna's wings. At the end of each wing is a narrow hinged surface called an aileron. Unlike the elevators on the tailplane which move in unison, the ailerons move in opposition, that is, one up, one down, and they control the aircraft in its roll axis. Back to our shaft again, this time passing through the aircraft from nose to tail. Picture the machine head-on in front view. Now imagine one wing dipping, rotating the aeroplane about the shaft. That is called rolling, or banking, and is governed by the ailerons via control wheel movement. Inboard from the ailerons are two larger surfaces called flaps. Unlike the elevators and ailerons, flaps do not raise above the fixed surface to which they are attached: they lower and retract back flush with the wing surface. Their purpose is to provide additional lift to the wing by altering the camber (curvature) of its airfoil surface, and also to create drag and thus act as aerodynamic brakes for slow flight or during the landing approach. Flaps can be manually operated via a simple mechanical linkage, or electrically activated, like those on the Cessna 152.

Let's climb aboard to view the Cessna's cockpit. There are two seats, side-by-side, and not overly generous on room for large-framed occupants. Ahead is the instrument panel, and projecting from it, dual control wheels. 'Wheels' is something of a misnomer in this case, because they are not round on most modern aircraft, but shaped like one half of a spectacle frame or like a flattened out letter 'W', and are often referred to as control yokes. Some training aircraft, usually those of British or European descent, still have the conventional control column, floor-mounted and hinged at its base, a 'joystick' in the old Royal Air Force jargon, but 'wheels' are much more common. They are mounted on shafts which slide in and out from the instrument panel, and the wheels also rotate, car-style, though over a much more limited 'lock-to-lock' range. They do not, however, steer the aeroplane on the ground, as almost all student pilots discover on their first flight when they wind the wheel energetically and wonder why the aeroplane refuses to follow its command.

The control wheel moves the elevators (back for up, forward for down) and the ailerons (wheel to the right to bank right and vice-versa). The rudder is controlled by a pair of pedals mounted in the footwell. Pushing on the left pedal applies left rudder and yaws the aircraft to the left, right pedal gives right rudder and right yaw. It is logical but not entirely natural; at first many student pilots feel a strong urge to try to slew the aircraft left or right as they would a soap-box go-cart, in exactly the opposite of the correct sense of rudder pedal movement. The rudder pedals are usually linked to a steerable nosewheel when the aircraft is on the ground. Steering when taxying or rolling for take-off or after landing is thus accomplished with the feet using both rudder and nosewheel. The rudder pedals may also operate brakes on the aircraft's mainwheels, though some trainers have hand-operated brakes, and all have a parking brake. On aircraft fitted with toe-brakes, pressure on the top of the rudder pedals operates the brakes, either in unison or individually (to assist in making a tight turn while taxying or parking, for example); they are sensitive and require much lighter pressures than the brake pedals in average family cars.

Remember the trim tab? It is operated by a trim wheel, which may be set on a central console or between the seats, as it is on our Cessna 152, or in the cabin roof area in the form of a handcrank as on some Piper Cherokee models. Trim wheels operate in the natural sense: forward movement of the wheel to trim nose down, backward to trim nose up, and are marked with a neutral position when the trim tab trails flush with the elevator surface. Other controls? There is a fuel selector which may have a simple on/off movement to allow the fuel to flow from the tanks in the wings, or it may also select individual (left/right) tanks as required. In simple high-wing aircraft such as the Cessna 152 fuel is fed to the engine by that most reliable device, gravity, so there are no fuel pumps to concern us. On low-wing types an electric fuel pump is used to ensure a constant flow of fuel during engine starting, take-off and landing, while an engine-driven fuel pump draws fuel in cruising flight.

There are three principal engine controls. The throttle

sets the required power, much like the accelerator pedal in a car, except that when flying you do not have to make constant adjustments as you might when driving. Once the desired power setting has been made, it is left until a change in flight configuration — a climb or descent, for instance — demands a new setting. Throttles are hand-operated and can take the form of a simple push-pull knob or a quadrant-mounted 'power lever'. Whichever the aircraft has (the Cessna 152's throttle is the push-pull type) the throttle control operates in the natural sense: forward to increase power, back to reduce it. A friction-nut or collar is provided which is tightened to hold the power setting required. The mixture control, readily identified by its red knob, controls the fuel/air mixture reaching the engine. During training flights it will most usually be found in the rich (fully forward) position. Leaning out the mixture (reducing the fuel/air ratio) confers greater fuel economy and smoother running at altitude but will not concern the student during the earliest training flights. When the mixture control is pulled fully back (or out from the instrument panel) it is in the 'idle cut-off' position: the engine will be starved of fuel and will soon stop. Mixture controls are moved to idle cut-off only when the aeroplane is on the ground and parked, or during airborne or ground emergencies when it may be necessary to cut off the flow of fuel to the engine, hence the cautionary red knob.

Thirdly there is a carburettor heat control, which is used to provide heated air to the carburettor to prevent ice forming in the carburettor intake and consequent loss of power which can occur under certain quite common climatic conditions. Carburettor heat controls again may take the form of push-pull knobs or levers. Unlike throttle and mixture controls, carburettor heat knobs are pulled out to function (hot air) and pushed in for off (ambient temperature air). Supplementary to these primary engine controls, but no less vital, is a magneto switch, marked off-left-right-both for the engine's dual ignition system. Each magneto is tested before flight; the 'both' position is used at all other times, and the magneto switch usually doubles as a starter switch by turning the aircraft's ignition key past the both position to start, just like a car. There is a plunger-type primer for priming the aircraft's engine before starting, usually necessary only when the engine is cold, as with a car's choke.

What about those banks of instruments? You are thinking of airliner cockpits which do have dozens of instruments seemingly scattered over every available piece of cockpit wall and roof, although these are increasingly being replaced by Electronic Flight Instrumentation System (EFIS) cathode ray tube (CRT) displays in the 'glass cockpits' of new generation transport aircraft. Such aircraft also have two or three highly trained crew members to monitor their instrument displays. A light training aeroplane's instrument array is much more modest.

There are three main types of instrument on the panel: Flight Instruments; Engine and System Instruments; and Navigational Instruments. We will look at each group individually.

The Flight Instruments are: Airspeed Indicator (ASI); Altimeter; Artificial Horizon; Vertical Speed Indicator (VSI); Turn-and-Slip Indicator; and Direction Indication (DI). The airspeed indicator is self-explanatory. It gives the aircraft's indicated airspeed in miles per hour or knots (nautical miles per hour). That is speed through the air, not over the ground, which will vary according to whether the aircraft is flying into a headwind or gaining the benefit of a tailwind. The airspeed indicator works by measuring the static pressure of (still) air surrounding the aircraft and comparing it with the dynamic pressure of air moving past the aircraft.

The altimeter also measures air pressure. It is essentially an aneroid barometer with an adjustable sub-scale on which is pre-set a known pressure value. In training you will soon become acquainted with two common pressure settings identified by the 'Q' Code, a form of abbreviation once commonly used in air-to-ground communications in the days of wireless telegraphy, but now mostly restricted to these and a few other common usages. The QFE is the local airfield pressure setting at which the altimeter will read zero when the aircraft is on the ground at the airfield, while the QNH is a sea level pressure setting at which the altimeter will indicate the airfield's elevation (height above sea level) when the aircraft is on the ground. Altimeters are calibrated in feet, with the adjustable sub-scale graduated in millibars, inches of mercury or hectopascals. An altimeter works on pressure differential, giving altitude above sea level or above the elevation of the airfield whose local pressure (QFE) has been set. It does not tell you your height above the ground over which you are flying. Thus if you fly over a hill which is 1,000 feet high with an altimeter reading 1,500 feet on the sea-level (QNH) pressure setting, your altitude will be 1,500 feet above sea level, but your height (or vertical clearance) above the hill is only 500 feet.

The vertical speed indicator measures the rate of pressure change as the aircraft ascends or descends, and presents this information in the form of a feet-per-minute up/down reading. The pressure instruments — ASI, altimeter and VSI — all suffer from slight lag in displaying information when airspeed, altitude or rate of climb or descent change. Inexperienced student pilots often find themselves impatiently chasing these instruments, making further corrections instead of waiting for the instrument indications to stabilise.

The artificial horizon operates on the gyroscope principle. It provides information about the aircraft's attitude relative to the horizon. The instrument's face comprises a replica aeroplane symbol combined with an horizon bar which moves to show the aircraft's relative position: climbing, diving, banking left or right, or in any combination. This instrument forms the basis of Instrument Flight when no outside visual references are available. The turn-and-slip indicator, also commonly known as the 'needle-and-ball', turn-and-bank indicator or turn co-ordinator, is a two-part instrument comprising a needle (miniature aeroplane symbol in modern turn co-ordinators) which deflects left or right as appropriate when the aeroplane banks into a turn, and a free-floating ball in a spirit level which remains centred when the aircraft is in a balanced or co-ordinated turn but moves sideways if the aircraft is slipping (sliding sideways into the direction of turn) or skidding (slithering outwards away from the direction of turn). Although it has been included in this section on flight instruments, the direction indicator is primarily a navigation instrument which indicates the aircraft's heading in degrees magnetic against a compass card.

The engine and system instruments in a small training aeroplane such as the Cessna 152 are few and quite straightforward, comprising usually a tachometer (rev counter) which indicates engine revolutions per minute; oil temperature and oil pressure gauges; an alternator gauge which measures electrical load (like an ammeter in a car); and a suction gauge, which monitors suction for the vacuum-driven gyro instruments. There are also fuel quantity gauges to give an indication of how much fuel remains in the aircraft's petrol tank(s), but as a prudent pilot you will always make a visual check of each tank's contents before flying, and monitor fuel consumption during each flight.

The most common navigation instrument is still the old-fashioned Magnetic Compass, usually a bubble-type instrument mounted high up on top of the instrument panel glareshield or in the upper part of the windscreen. Magnetic compasses are slow responding and are subject to acceleration errors and regional magnetic influence, hence the use of the Direction Indicator or Directional Gyro (above) for more precise navigation. However, the DI must be synchronised with the aircraft's magnetic compass before take-off and at regular intervals throughout a flight. Later in training students encounter two further navigational instruments: the Automatic Direction Finder (ADF) and the VHF Omnidirectional Range (VOR) receiver. The ADF is a radio compass whose indicator needle points to the non-directional radio ground station transmitter to which it is tuned. The VOR receives signals from ground stations which transmit their signals along each of the 360 degrees of the compass or 'radials' as they are known. By tuning to a VOR ground station within range (VHF is a strictly line-of-sight aid) and selecting a desired radial a pilot can fly directly to (or away from) the station by keeping the VOR indicator needle centred in the instrument display.

Communications? All modern training aircraft have a VHF transceiver for communicating with airfield control towers and other air traffic control ground facilities. Some aircraft are equipped with cabin speakers for listening and a hand-held microphone for speaking, but individual headsets with boom microphones are preferable since they not only permit exchanges between pupil and instructor to be heard easily via an intercom facility, but effectively exclude some of the engine and airflow noise which unfortunately is an all too noticeable feature of light aeroplanes. With headsets you transmit to ground stations by pressing a 'push-to-talk' switch conveniently set into the hand-grip of each control wheel.

Does it still sound daunting? Probably, if you are entirely unfamiliar with aeroplanes, but rest assured that it will all seem much clearer when you see the aircraft's controls and instruments actually working.

If you are still game to try (and you should be), read on. . .

Chapter 2
The Private Pilot

The minimum basic licensing requirement for flying powered aeroplanes without supervision is the Private Pilot Licence, popularly called the PPL. It is broadly equivalent to a full driving licence, permitting the holder to fly private aeroplanes for personal business and pleasure and to carry passengers provided no payment is received. This, and certain other restrictions, will be dealt with in greater detail later.

A PPL (Aeroplanes) or PPL (Helicopters) is therefore the starting point for virtually all non-commercial civil flying except gliding, hang gliding and microlight flying, which have their own systems of pilot qualification and are outside the scope of this book. No general academic qualifications are demanded. There is no lower age limit at which you may start learning to fly, but to apply for the issue of a licence (and to be cleared to fly solo while training) you must be at least 17 years of age. There is no upper age limit. Many people in their sixties have successfully completed PPL training courses.

However, unlike the driving licence, which can be obtained by taking any haphazard form of tuition which will get an applicant through the test, a PPL is granted only after completion of a recognised syllabus of ground and flight instruction conducted by properly qualified flying instructors, and after successful passes have been obtained in ground examinations and flying tests.

Although a pilot friend or relative may be able to give you some basic experience at the controls or an aeroplane, such experience cannot be counted towards the minimum number of hours required for the PPL course unless he or she is a qualified flying instructor.

The licensing of pilots in the United Kingdom is the responsibility of the Civil Aviation Authority (CAA), whose records show that there are approximately 27,000 active PPL holders in the country, with some 2,500 new licences being issued annually.

The CAA syllabus for the Private Pilot Licence calls for a minimum of 40 hours of flying instruction. This is strictly a statutory minimum requirement and does not guarantee (indeed it would be unusual) that a licence is automatically won at the 40th hour. In practice some 55–60 hours of instruction is the average qualifying time for *ab initio* students, a fact to keep in mind when calculating the likely cost of obtaining your licence.

So you think you would like to become a private pilot? What to do? Where to go?
There are more than 200 flying schools, clubs and training organisations in the United Kingdom. They vary in size from chummy one-man, one-aeroplane businesses to large operations with fleets of a dozen or more aircraft, staffs of full-time instructors on call seven days a week and comprehensive facilities on the ground for classroom study.

What you are taught should not vary, because the training syllabuses, examinations and tests are standardised. But *how* you are taught, the rate at which you progress, how much you pay, and whether you get good value for your money will depend on wise selection of your training school (and a modicum of luck in all probability). Big doesn't necessarily mean best, nor small cheapest. A one-man outfit may well provide a very personal touch, but consider what may happen to the continuity of your training if that one man goes sick, or his one aeroplane is grounded for a protracted period of maintenance.

How to go about choosing? A selection of clubs and flight schools is listed in the Appendices. The Aircraft Owners & Pilots Association (AOPA) can also supply a directory of their member clubs, and a very comprehensive *Where to Fly Guide* containing courses offered, aircraft fleets and membership and flying charges is published annually in the April issue of *Pilot* magazine.

As a first step, get one of these lists and search out the operators in your area. How far you cast your net is up to you. Do not assume that the school nearest you must be the one to choose. You might have an airfield and a flying club/ school within a mile or two of your home. Ideal? Not necessarily. Much of your training will involve general handling in clear airspace. If your 'local' airfield is a commercial airport with its own protected airspace you will have to spend time at the beginning and end of each lesson flying to and from a practice area: all good experience, but it will be costing you money in flying time during which you will not be progressing through the exercises of the PPL syllabus. At a busy airport you may also find yourself frequently waiting in a line of traffic to take-off. Since charges for flying lessons are often costed from engine start to engine stop (or 'brakes off' to 'brakes on'), this can be a very expensive and unproductive traffic jam. Airfields where many flying clubs and schools operate will also create traffic problems when it comes to the 'circuits and bumps' part of the PPL course when you will spend hours doing nothing but taking off, flying around the rectangular course of the airfield's circuit, landing, taking off . . . At a busy airfield other traffic may seriously limit the number of circuits which can be flown in an hour's lesson.

On the other hand, a busy airfield environment with a mix of commercial and private traffic will quickly breed confidence in radio and air traffic procedures.

Having selected likely airfields within your reach, list the training establishments at each and pay them a visit. Don't be daunted if the airfield entrance is dotted with *keep out* or *pilots only* signs threatening dire peril to trespassers: they are to keep out small boys with inquisitive fingers. Weekends are invariably busy if the weather is reasonable, and thus a good time to gain an impression of flying school activity, but you may not get the fullest attention from staff when they are busiest. A weekday visit would probably be better for asking questions, getting an escorted tour of facilities and looking over aircraft.

Flying is still very much an enthusiast's activity in Britain. An increasing number of flying clubs and schools (perhaps the majority) have plush, sparkling premises with smartly-dressed staff, airy classrooms and comfortable lounges, but more than a few still operate from buildings left behind by the services after the war, with facilities sometimes little improved in the meanwhile. Whether you select a small homely club or a large flying training school is largely a matter of personal preference.

You can learn a great deal from the reception you get on your first visit. Does anyone bother to ask if they can help you, for a start? Flying does generate legendary camaraderie among fellow pilots, but sad to say strangers are not universally accorded warm welcomes, even from those very people whose business it is to win over new customers.

If your reception is too offhand, go somewhere else where they want your business. Otherwise, explain that you think you might like to learn to fly and could someone answer a few questions?

How many training aeroplanes are there? This can be very important. With, say, just two on the fleet, the chances of lessons being delayed or cancelled through technical faults or because the last pilot did not return the aircraft on time can be very high. Does the school have its own, or readily-available, maintenance facilities to ensure aircraft reliability and availability? How many instructors are there, and what is the student/instructor ratio? Is there an efficient system for booking lessons, one that will ensure you get the instructor you want?

At private pilot level flying instruction is not a well-paid profession. As a result, the instructional staff at many clubs and schools is made up of young aspiring professional pilots building hours towards their Commercial Pilots Licences (see Chapter 3). There is nothing wrong with this practice except that it results in a rapid turnover among instructors which in turn leads to discontinuity in training. An occasional change of tutor can be refreshing, but having a different instructor for every other lesson is a frustrating and expensive business as you find yourself going over some parts of the PPL course time after time while never touching others. It is unlikely that many schools could guarantee one-to-one instruction from the same instructor throughout a PPL course, but one which has a good number of older full-time professional flying instructors on staff should score highly one your list of possibles. Ask also how many of the training staff are Qualified Flying Instructors (QFIs), and how many are Assistant Flying Instructors (AFIs). QFIs are the more experienced and are essential to 'sign you off' at certain stages of the syllabus (first solo, for example), so check carefully how many are on the staff and how often they are available.

Ask to see the ground training facilities. Are there proper classrooms, lecture rooms, or at least individual briefing cubicles for study and for pre- and post-flight discussions with your instructor? Does the school run classes, which may be evening lecture sessions, for the PPL examination subjects? Ground school is just as important as flying on the road to gaining a PPL. There is nothing worse than trying to master complex theory or solve a tricky navigational problem in a noisy office with telephone ringing or in a club bar surrounded by chattering pilots and beeping video games machines or one-armed bandits.

Note also if the whole operation seems to be run in an efficient and businesslike manner. Are the premises and aircraft clean and well cared for? It is not unreasonable to assume that a seedy and run-down operation may adopt a similarly careless attitude to training you. You may well get your licence eventually, but it will have cost more and taken longer than it should have.

If possible try to talk with other students at the school. Ask what they think of it, and how they have progressed with their training. Don't believe everything you hear. Every activity has its share of professional moaners who can find fault with everyone and everything, but a high proportion of complaints should be taken as a warning that all may not be well.

Trial lessons
Most flying schools offer trial lessons, and you should take advantage of this, at least at those which seem to meet all other requirements. Do not be alarmed at the term 'trial'. It is flying that is on trial, not you. The purpose of the flight is (or should be) to acquaint you with the sensations of flight in small aircraft and to demonstrate the basic effects of the aeroplane's controls, not to decide whether you have the makings of a pilot.

A trial lesson (sometimes called an air experience flight) usually lasts about 30 minutes, and typically will cost around £50. An extension of this idea is the Acorne Sporting Starts scheme which offers gift vouchers for trial flights which are redeemable at any of 35 participating flying schools throughout the country. Voucher-holders receive a flight training audio cassette, pilot's logbook, clipboard, flight certificate, personal insurance and one or more (according to voucher value) training flights in a light aircraft. Details of this scheme can be obtained from Acorne, PO Box 1057, Marlow, Buckinghamshire SL7 3XT, telephone 0494 451703.

However you go about booking your trial flight, a considerate school will arrange your first light aeroplane trip on a calm day with good visibility, free of gusting winds, turbulence or low cloud which are not good introductions to flying. The lesson should be exactly that — an introduction to piloting following a preflight briefing on what you are going to do in the air, with you handling the controls under the instructor's supervision for some of the time. If you get no more than a sightseeing ride with the instructor remaining steadfastly silent and not relinquishing the controls for a moment, suspect the worst of the school concerned.

Several facts will quickly emerge during your trial flight. Flying in a light aeroplane is not at all like riding in the claustrophobic confines of a large airliner. You will fly much lower and enjoy a fine panoramic view of the world denied those who can only peer through a few square inches of an airliner's window. You will however discover also that the cockpits of two-seat training aeroplanes are noisy and often cramped places which makes them poor classrooms in which to absorb theory, further emphasising the need for proper ground study facilities at the school where your instructor can brief you in peace and quiet. The use of headsets with an intercom when flying overcomes some of the problems of effective instructor/student communication, and also reduces the fatiguing effects of engine noise.

Still keen to become a pilot?
Now is the time to talk to your selected school about booking a course of lessons for the Private Pilot Licence syllabus.

Because of the number of hours needed to qualify for a PPL varies among the individuals, most schools provide flying tuition on an hourly basis rather than signing up students for a complete course from the outset. Some do however offer fixed-price courses: check first if this is a guaranteed get-your-licence deal. It may be that the course fee only includes the statutory minimum of 40 hours' flying, which will almost certainly not be enough. Otherwise you pay as you go, usually at an hourly rate (or pro rata) against the time from engine start to engine stop. Dual flying (that is, with an instructor) usually comes a little more expensive than solo use of an aircraft, typically by a few pounds more per hour, though many schools now adopt a higher 'training' charge rate throughout a course, irrespective of whether the student is accompanied by an instructor or flying solo.

How much will it cost? Hourly charges vary from school to school, for different aircraft, of different ages, and in different geographical locations. In late 1990 a typical hourly charge for dual instruction in a Cessna 152 or Piper Tomahawk class of aircraft, including VAT, was around £65, but it can be considerably higher in the London area, for example. On the assumption that it will take some 55 hours or thereabouts to complete the course, a sum of £3,500 should therefore be regarded as the likely cost of the flying element of a PPL course. Add medical examination fees, the cost of books, maps and ancillary equipment, examination and flight test charges and the licence issue fee and £4,000 is a realistic assessment of total outlay. You will find PPL courses offered for much less, but whatever rate you are quoted, do determine exactly what the charge includes. It is not unknown for schools to attract business by offering seemingly generous hourly rates while neglecting to point out that they do not include such non-optional extras as preflight briefings, instructor's time, airport landing fees and VAT.

Some schools will arrange personal loans through finance companies to pay for flying tuition. Some also accept popular credit cards for payment. And it is not unknown for understanding bank managers to offer loans for lessons. It is worth asking a school if they give discounts for block bookings (say, ten hours) of instruction paid for in advance, although in general it is not wise to part with too large a sum in advance, lest you should decide to give up before completing the course, or — as has happened to a number of unfortunate students — the school goes out of business.

You may be asked to become a member of the school or club. This is a normal insurance prerequisite for flying their aeroplanes, and takes the form of a one-time joining fee and annual subscription which entitles you to make use of all the club's facilities and join in social activities. Most clubs also offer family or social membership for spouses, children and friends which will enable them to fly as passengers in club aircraft. Apart from flying, you will find that most clubs and schools also cater for social activities, and many have a bar, strictly for *after* flying drinking.

We mentioned insurance. Do check that the operator holds appropriate aircraft and liability cover which indemnifies you against claims should you be unfortunate enough to have an accident or incident while flying. A reputable school will be happy to assure you on this point and provide evidence of cover. It is important. Even a relatively minor incident on the ground can do very expensive damage to aircraft; a crash involving other people, aircraft or property could result in potentially ruinous claims. And be sure to tell your own insurance company that you are learning to fly. Life insurance policies often contain an exclusion clause restricting coverage to fare-paying passenger flying on commercial airlines, or words to that effect. Cover for private flying can usually be obtained for a very small increase in premium. If your insurance company tries to tell you otherwise, look for another one.

Are you fit enough to be a pilot?

Although you do not have to meet any medical standards before starting to learn to fly, before you can fly a powered aeroplane solo (and thus before you can obtain your PPL) you must have a valid medical certificate, which also doubles as a Student Pilot's Licence and therefore should be obtained before you start training.

Contrary to popular myth you do not have to be superfit astronaut material to become a pilot. While it is undeniable that airline and military pilots are required to maintain very high levels of physical fitness which are constantly monitored, the Class III medical certificate needed for a PPL sets much less demanding standards. To obtain a medical certificate you must undergo an examination by a doctor who is authorised by the Civil Aviation Authority to carry out such tests. Unless he or she *is* a CAA Authorised Medical Examiner your local general practitioner cannot conduct the examination. However, there is a very good geographic spread of AMEs throughout the country. Most large towns have one. Your flying school should be able to give you a list of those practising in the area.

The medical examination (which has to be paid for at the time — fees vary according to doctor and depth of examination required) is quite straightforward. You will first be asked to complete CAA Medical Form 46, a personal health questionnaire detailing significant medical conditions from which you may have suffered. Although the relevance of some of its questions may not be apparent, the form should be completed as fully and truthfully as you are able. The doctor will check eyesight, hearing, reflexes, respiratory system and blood pressure, among other things. For applicants aged 40 years or over a resting electrocardiogram is required, usually necessitating a hospital visit.

If all is well your Medical Certificate/Student Pilot's Licence will normally be issued straight away. A Class III certificate is valid for five years of those aged under 40 (or up to 42 if issued close to the 40th year); two years for 40–50 year olds; one year for 50–70 year olds; and for six months after the 70th birthday. The ECG examination is required for renewal of the certificate every four years between the ages of 40–50, every two years between 50–60 years, annually between 60–70 years and every six months for those over 70 years.

All licensed pilots must hold a current medical certificate for their licence to remain valid, and must inform the CAA in writing of any injury or medical condition might invalidate the certificate. Ladies may like to note that pregnancy automatically invalidates a medical certificate until after the birth, when another medical examination must be made before a certificate can be reissued.

Generally speaking anyone in good health and of average fitness should have no problem passing the PPL medical examination, but there are certain complaints such as epilepsy, diabetes requiring medication for control, and cardiac problems which normally preclude the granting of a medical certificate. For this reason (and because some disqualifying conditions may not be known to the would-be-pilot) it is essential to apply for a medical certificate before starting training. If you should be among those unfortunate few who cannot meet the requirements, you will not have wasted money on flying lessons. Eyesight defects which are correctable with spectacles or contact lenses are usually acceptable. In such cases the medical certificate will probably be endorsed with a requirement for the holder to carry a spare pair of spectacles when flying as a guard against loss or breakage in the air.

Loss of limbs or other physical impairment does not automatically exclude one from becoming a private pilot. Many paraplegics have successfully gained their licenses, indeed there is an annual sponsorship scheme (see below) which provides PPL training for the disabled. The criterion is that a disabled pilot must be able to operate all the aircraft's controls fully. Adapted aircraft controls which enable, for example, the rudder to be operated by hand instead of the feet may be acceptable providing control movement is not restricted. Quick-conversion kits to modify aircraft for disabled pilots have been developed for many common training types. The CAA Medical Branch examines each disabled applicant for a PPL medical certificate on merit. Far from being ogres, the staff are most anxious to assist anyone with medical problems to get into the air if it is possible within the constraints of safety.

The PPL Course

We have already noted that the course for the Private Pilot's Licence is of a minimum 40 hours' duration. It must be conducted to a syllabus which has been recognised by the CAA and comprises an integrated programme of flying and ground tuition. The school or club is required to keep detailed records of each student's progress to ensure that training has been carried out systematically.

Full details of the United Kingdom PPL Syllabus is contained in the Civil Aviation Authority booklet *CAP 53 — The Private Pilot's Licence and Associated Ratings*, which is essential reading for any aspiring PPL (see Bibliography). Briefly, the recognised syllabus minima call for a minimum of 20 hours' dual instruction including four hours each on pilot navigation and instrument flying; and a minimum of ten hours of solo flying which must include at least four hours cross-country flying as a pilot-in-command during the nine months preceding application for a licence, to include a cross-country flight visiting two aerodromes, one of which must be at least 50 nautical miles distant from home base. *(Note: syllabus requirements do change from time to time. Since books often remain in print for long periods it is essential to check with the CAA on the latest requirements and supplements to CAP 53.)*

Flight Training is divided into a sequence of numbered exercises:

1.	Aircraft Familiarisation
1E.	Emergency Drills
2.	Preparation for and Action after Flight
3.	Air Experience
4.	Effects of Controls and Further Effects
5.	Taxying
6.	Straight and Level Flight
7.	Climbing
8.	Descending
9.	Turning
10A.	Slow Flight, Stalling
10B.	Stalling, Spin Awareness
12.	Take-off and Climb to the Downwind Position
12E.	Engine Failure after take-off, Circuit
13.	Approach and Landing, and Going Around
14.	First Solo Flight
15.	Advanced Turning
17A & B.	Forced Landing, Precautionary Landing
18A.	Pilot Navigation, Compass Turns and Map Reading
18B, C, E, G.	Dual Navigation
18D, F.	Solo Navigation Flight Test
18I.	Qualifying Cross-country Flight
19.	Instrument Appreciation and Flying

General Flight Test

You will have noticed Exercise 14 — *First Solo Flight*, that unrepeatable moment, the highpoint of every pilot's life from neophyte to airline captain, when first you are in sole command of an aeroplane. When will you go solo? As soon as your instructor thinks you are ready, not before. You must hold a medical certificate and have passed the Air Law examination before you solo. Most students are sent off on their first solo circuit of the airfield when they have completed 10–12 hours of dual instruction, but there is no set time in the syllabus, and going solo does not — contrary to popular belief — mean that you have gained your wings and become a pilot. Far from it. It is a confidence-building exercise which assures you that your instructor has faith that you can take off, fly around the airfield circuit pattern, land and cope with any likely emergencies which might occur. Nothing more. Just when that golden moment comes and you write 'First Solo' in your pilot's logbook (usually in unnecessarily large and occasionally shaky handwriting) depends mostly on your own ability and rate of learning, so take no notice of 'experts' who tell you that unless you go solo in x number of hours you stand no chance of gaining your licence. You may be sure that if you go on too long before showing signs of reaching solo standard your instructor will tell you.

How long will the PPL course take? Again, it depends on a number of factors, perhaps most important of which is how frequently you take your lessons. Continuity is vitally important in any learning process, no more so than in flying, and in the early stages it will certainly determine how quickly you go solo. Long gaps between lessons will invariably mean spending a period of each detail re-learning something forgotten from the previous session, and must increase the duration and cost of the entire course.

If possible try to fly at least once a week, preferably more frequently. Best of all, if you are able to set aside a period of two or three weeks, flying each day as weather permits, you should be able to cover a substantial portion of the syllabus quite quickly. Bear in mind, though, that flying instruction (indeed all light aircraft operation) is very weather dependent. Lucky is the student in the United Kingdom who does not have a few lessons cancelled because of unsuitable conditions. It is frustrating, but you will have to learn to live with it. Aeroplanes also have a habit of developing niggling faults just as you are about to fly. It is therefore inadvisable to try to fit a flying lesson into a day on which you have a busy programme of work or social commitments. Better to set aside an entire day and schedule several lessons, with time between each for ground study of the exercises to be flown. You can help keep the school's schedule running smoothly by always arriving in plenty of time for preflight briefings from your instructor and for checking the aircraft before flying. If you have to cancel for any reason, do try to give as much advance notice as possible so that the aeroplane and instructor can be allocated to another student. Next time it could be you waiting to fit in another hour's flying.

Some flying schools offer full-time residential courses for the PPL, which aim to complete the course within a few weeks. An excellent idea providing you can spare the time and money, with the *caveat* that the British weather is an unwelcome and often uncooperative intruder into the best organised courses.

Gound School
The Ground Training element of the PPL syllabus covers the following Technical Subjects:
Air Legislation
Navigation
Meteorology
Principles of Flight
Airframes and Aero Engines
Airworthiness
Aircraft Instruments
Aircraft Type (the specific model of aeroplane used in your
  training)
Fire, First Aid and Safety Equipment
Aviation Medicine
Ground training, or ground school, is an important (and statutorily required) part of the PPL syllabus which must be closely coordinated with flying training so that the relevant subjects and procedures have been covered on the ground before they are put into practice in the air. The minimum recommended amount of formal classroom tuition is a mere 15 hours, but in practice a considerable amount of additional study will be needed to prepare for the PPL examinations which must be passed before a licence is issued. Once again it is difficult to put a precise figure on the time needed, since it varies according to the student's ability to learn, but 50–100 hours is accepted as an average figure.

Although pre- and post-flight briefings from your instructor should be an essential part of each flying lesson, few flying schools offer one-to-one teaching for the ground examinations, unless you are prepared to pay for an instructor's time to give you individual tuition. Most offer lecture courses for

Cessna 150s and 152s are popular two-seat trainers, widely used by British flying schools. (Author)

All-composite construction Slingsby T67M Firefly II, used by a number of PPL and Commercial schools for basic and advanced flying training.
(John Dignan, Slingsby Aviation)

Instrument panel of Cessna 172, typical of modern light aircraft cockpits. (Cessna)

Cessna 172 Skyhawk is the world's best-selling light aircraft, used for training and touring by many flying schools. (Author)

American Piper Warrior (above) and French Robin 400 (below) are four-seaters, equally suited to training and touring. (Author)

Glider towing may be performed by holders of Basic Commercial Pilots Licences. It is one way of building flying hours and experience. (Author)

A Night Rating is often the first 'step up' for private fliers afters gaining their PPLs. (Author)

groups of student pilots, often conducted as evening classes, for which a separate, usually modest, charge is made. Audio-visual courses using video and aural tapes are also employed. Some polytechnics and further education centres may also offer tuition, and a few schools run week-long or weekend intensive ground school courses that cover the entire PPL ground school syllabus, including sitting the Technical Examinations, with on-site accommodation available if required. There are also available a number of home study courses, including audio tapes covering all the PPL subjects — an excellent idea which can be put to good use on car stereo players when making long journeys, or travelling to and from the airfield for lessons — see Bibliography.

Your progress through the PPL course will be monitored by the school. The CAA recommend schools to issue students with copies of their syllabus which he or she can sign in completion of each phase of training, agreeing that the item(s) has been covered. You will also keep a record of your flying hours in your Personal Flying Logbook which every student must submit with the licence application at the end of the course. Your logbook is an important document — the only official record of your flying time — which must be maintained throughout your flying life

The Tests
Before you can apply for a Private Pilot's Licence you must pass written and oral examinations and take practical tests.

The examinations consist of written papers on the Technical subjects: *Airframes and Engines; Aviation Law, Flights Rules and Procedures; Navigation;* and *Meteorology*, and an oral technical quiz on the specific aircraft type on which you have trained. The written examination questions are of the multiple choice type, e.g. *Flaps are fitted to aircraft to: (a) Increase lift and drag while lowering stalling speed; (b) Increase drag, payload and stalling angle; or (c) Increase lift, drag and stalling speed.* (The correct answer is *(a)*.

The Technical Examinations and oral test are usually taken at your flying school. An hour is allocated for completion of each subject, with a minimum pass mark for each paper of 70 per cent. You do not have to sit all the examinations at one time, thus only those in which you fail to attain the pass mark have to be re-sat. The CAA recommend that *Aviation Law, Flight Rules and Procedures* should be passed before making the first solo flight, and those in *Navigation* and *Meteorology* (and the test for a Flight Radiotelephony Operator's licence — see below) before making the first solo cross-country flight.

The practical tests comprise a Navigation Flight Test (NFT), and the General Flying Test (GFT), which is the final hurdle before the issue of your licence.

The Navigation Flight Test comprises a flight of some one and a half hours' duration over a triangular route during which an examiner assesses the student pilot's flight planning; handling of air traffic control instructions; dead reckoning navigation; map reading; ability to maintain course, altitude and airspeed at normal and low levels; and ability to establish position visually after disruption of the planned flight, and to carry out a practice diversion to an alternative destination in simulated poor weather conditions. The NFT is a pass or fail test, all elements of which must be successfully completed in a single flight, or the test re-taken in its entirety.

Once the NFT has been completed you can make your Qualifying Solo Cross-Country flight, which consists of a triangular journey with two landings at airfields away from base, one of which must be at least 50 nautical miles distant from your starting point. Controllers at the airfields visited sign a landing card to confirm your visit, and are also invited to observe and comment on circuit discipline and landing procedure.

The General Flying Test, as its name implies, examines the student's competence in the Exercises of the PPL flying syllabus, any (or all) of which you may be asked to demonstrate to the examiner's satisfaction during a flight lasting about one hour. Should you fail, the examiner will advise you of those aspects of your flying which need refining, and after some further dual instruction and practice you can take the GFT again.

Most larger flying schools have a CAA-delegated examiner on staff, usually a senior instructor or the Chief Flying Instructor (CFI), so unlike the driving test you do not have to apply months in advance to take your PPL GFT.

For student pilots, learning to fly also means mastering the use of the aircraft's VHF radio transmitter for two-way communication with airport control towers and other air traffic control facilities on the ground. Radiotelephony (RT) training is an integral part of the PPL syllabus, and leads to a test for the issue of a Flight Radiotelephony Operator (FRTO) licence, popularly known as the RT Licence, which is a seperate document to the PPL. A student pilot must therefore learn the language of aviation. Not the *Tally-Ho!*, *Angels One-Five, Roger, wilco, over-and-out* banter of poor quality flying films, but the precise language of air traffic control which has two functions: to convey the maximum information in the fewest words, and to avoid ambiguity which could lead to misunderstandings and thence to accidents.

So we use *Affirm* for Yes, *Negative* for No, and the phonetic alphabet (*A:Alpha, B:Bravo* and so on). Once you overcome microphone nerves and learn to relax you should slip into the correct phraseology without stumbling over your words. Books and cassette tapes are available to teach RT technique. You might also find an airband VHF radio useful for tuning to airport and ATC frequencies to get the feel of radio procedures. A written examination and practical RT test (again usually conducted by your flying school) must be passed before an RT licence is issued, although instructors' certification of practical inflight RT training, and assessment of competence during the NFT and GFT, may be accepted in lieu of the practical test at schools lacking RT testing facilities.

The Licence
Once you have completed your PPL course, Technical Examinations, Navigation Flight Test, Qualifying Solo Cross-Country flight and General Flight Test, your examiner will send off your examination results, Personal Flying Logbook and PPL application form to the Civil Aviation Authority, who will enter a Certificate of Test in your logbook and return it with your brand-new Private Pilot Licence.

The licence (not a grand document, unfortunately, but a computer-generated fold-out sheet in a plastic wallet) is non-expiring. Yours for life. However, to maintain the validity of the licence — to 'keep it current' as we say — you must revalidate it by having a Certificate of Experience entered in your logbook, confirming that you have completed a minimum of five hours flying experience in the 13 months preceding each 'signing off'. Of the five hours, at least three must have been logged as pilot-in-command without supervision. The remainder may be as pilot-in-command under supervision (PIC U/S) with a qualified instructor or authorised examiner on check flights or tests, or dual flying instruction with a qualified instructor provided that at the end of the flights the instructor signed your logbook to certify your competency to fly unsupervised. If you hold a licence which permits you to fly different groups of aircraft (multi-engine, helicopters — see below) you must have completed five hours in 13 months in each group of aircraft for each to be revalidated.

In practice, five hours of flying in 13 months is not enough to make you a safe or proficient pilot. If you do not fly as pilot-in-command for a period of more than 25 months you must undergo further training and take another flight test to revalidate your licence.

The validity of the PPL also depends on possession of a current medical certificate. If your certificate expires, or you fail a renewal examination, your PPL automatically becomes invalid until such time as a medical certificate is reissued.

Many non-fliers suppose that a Private Pilot's Licence gives you carte blanche to fly any aircraft. No so. Its provisions are quite specific. If, as is most likely, the licence is issued for Group A [PPL(A)], you may only fly single-engined landplanes weighing less than 12,500lbs. That gives a broad scope of aircraft types which you could, in theory, fly quite legally. But in practice if you are hiring aeroplanes from the club or school where you learned to fly, you are likely to be restricted to the aircraft type(s) on which you trained, or something very similar in terms of performance, complexity and handling, until you have gained more experience. Insurance premiums (or the availability of cover) are likely to impose similar constraints even if you buy your own aircraft.

If you then want to move up to more complex types you will need further dual instruction and a check-out by an instructor or someone familiar with the aircraft before setting off alone.

There are other restrictions to the basic PPL. You may not fly on the Airways which are the 'motorways' of the air traffic system, must remain in sight of the earth's surface (not in or above cloud) and with a minimum inflight visibility of one-and-a-half nautical miles. The detailed privileges and exemptions pertaining to the PPL are many, and cannot be repeated in depth here. *CAP 53 The Private Pilot's Licence* gives the fullest information and should always be consulted for specific details.

Can you carry passengers? Certainly, provided they do not pay you in cash (or anything which could conceivably be converted into cash) for your services as a pilot. The PPL is strictly an amateur licence in the literal sense, specifically forbidding flying for 'valuable consideration', although the acceptance of awards or prizes in amateur flying events such as races or rallies is permitted, as is cost-sharing between a pilot and no more than three passengers if all (including the pilot) pay an equal share and are members of the same flying club or group, and reimbursement by an employer of actual costs incurred in using a private aircraft for business trips.

You can fly abroad with a PPL. The CAA licence is widely recognised. If you are flying a British-registered aeroplane there should be no problem operating in foreign countries provided you comply with all the necessary Customs, Immigration and air traffic procedures. If you want to hire a foreign-registered aeroplane while abroad you will need to validate your British PPL for the country in question. This should be done in advance, since the time needed can vary from a few minutes' form filling to six months of negotiation, depending on which country you are dealing with. You will probably have to take an examination in local air law and have a check-ride with the operator hiring you the aeroplane.

Check-rides are also necessary in Britain if you want to hire an aircraft from a club where you and your experience level are not known, or at you local club if you have not flown recently. Just how recently you must have flown varies from club to club. Some insist on a check-out with an instructor (which you must of course pay for) if you have not flown within a month, so there is a further spur to keep in regular flying practice.

Helicopters
The foregoing summary of private pilot training is directed principally at those seeking to learn to fly fixed-wing light aeroplanes for the issue of a PPL (Aeroplanes).

It is, however, possible to learn to fly from scratch on helicopters, for the PPL (Helicopters). The course duration is a minimum of 40 hours, as with fixed-wing aircraft, and the examinations and testing requirements are also identical, although certain items of the flying syllabus vary to incorporate those exercises specifically related to rotary-winged flight and to omit manoeuvres (stalling for example) which cannot be performed in helicopters.

Helicopter flying training schools are becoming increasingly common. The cost of helicopter operation is much greater than that for light aircraft, although the popularity of light piston engined helicopters — particularly the two-seat Robinson R22 which is widely used for rotary-winged training in the UK — has helped reduce the cost of obtaining a PPL(H). At 1990 rates you could expect to pay around £200 per hour for instruction on a Robinson R22, and at least twice that figure for flying a turbine-engined Bell JetRanger.

The CAA permits holders of aeroplane licences (except Group D microlights) to reduce the minimum experience requirement to 35 hours on helicopters if adding a PPL(H) to their qualifications. A similar five-hour reduction also applies to helicopter pilots seeking a fixed-wing PPL.

Training abroad
Recent years have seen tremendous growth in the number of companies offering overseas 'package' training courses. These are mostly based in the United States, and to a lesser extent France, where more dependable weather can increase the chances of completing a PPL course within a specific period of time, typically three/four weeks.

At least two British operators offer courses in France (see appendices), one based at Cannes, the other at La Rochelle on the Atlantic coast. The advantage that these offer over most of the American schools is that their courses lead to the granting of a British CAA PPL, rather than an American Federal Aviation Administration certificate, so you return fully qualified to fly in the UK. It is also possible on these courses to undertake the ground school part of the course and take the CAA examinations before going to France to start the practical side of the syllabus, thus freeing more time for cramming those vital 40 flying hours into three weeks; indeed, some students have successfully completed the course in two weeks.

The attractions of the United States for taking a PPL course are principally cost and weather. Flight training and aircraft hire are much cheaper in the USA than in the UK or Europe, so it is possible for operators to offer packages that include ground and flight training, exams, accommodation, return airline fares and sometimes car hire for figures that may be below the cost of flight training alone at home. Typical rates being quoted by US package operators in late 1990 were around £2,000–£2,250 for a PPL course, all included.

US schools popular with overseas students tend to be in the southern states, Florida and Texas being particularly popular, where there's a good chance the weather will be suitable for flying most days, so rapid progress should be possible and completion of the course quite feasible within three or four weeks, perhaps less if you learn quickly, pick the right school and instructor, have good luck with the weather and everything goes as advertised.

Sounds too good to be true? There are drawbacks. For the most part these courses are for a US Federal Aviation Admistration licence, not British CAA PPL. You will need an FAA medical certificate before you go, but this can be done in Britain (the FAA office at the US Embassy, 5 Upper Grosvenor Street, London W1A 2JB can supply a list of FAA AMEs). Your FAA PPL can be validated for use in the UK when you get back home and you may continue to fly quite legally, but the FAA requires pilots with under 400 hours total flying time to take an annual flight review with an examiner, and thereafter a biennial review (neither are yet required by the CAA), which means that you will either have to seek out a UK-based FAA-designated examiner (and there are some) or return to the United States for your check-ride when the time comes around.

The alternative, which is probably wiser bearing in mind that American and British air traffic control systems and operating procedures differ considerably, that our airspace is generally much more congested and restricted, and that the clear blue skies of Florida are no preparation for British weather, is to convert your FAA PPL to a CAA one. The CAA is prepared to do this providing you can meet certain requirements. First you must send the FAA Temporary Airman Certificate which will have been issued by your examiner in the USA, your medical certificate, logbook and a fee for assessment by the Flight Crew Licensing Branch at Gatwick Airport. If all is well, you must then sit the UK Air Law examination, take an RT test and pay for the issue of your British licence. Ground tuition at a UK school will probably be necessary preparation for the examinations and tests. You would be wise also to take some dual flying instruction to familiarise yourself with UK procedures. If you plan to hire aircraft from a British club or school they will almost certainly require this anyway. All of this will add to the cost of getting your PPL in the United States, but it does give you valid licences for both countries — a great asset if you plan to take holidays or do further training or experience gathering in America.

While most operators offering package courses abroad are honest and endeavour to provide a good service, there have been sorry instances of students finding themselves having to pay substantially for hidden 'extras' after arriving in the United States, or that promised accommodation or training was not up to standard. Since most of these operators require full payment in advance of travelling to the USA you would be well advised to make careful enquiries of any school whose offers you are tempted to accept. At the very least ask for a list of satisfied British students who have trained at the school and contact them for their experiences. If a school can't (or won't) provide such a list, go elsewhere. Ensure also just what you are getting for your money. Are state taxes, examination fees and insurance indemnity included? If car hire is offered, does it include the cost of a collision damage waiver?

Some courses guarantee to get you and your licence for the quoted fee, regardless of how many flying hours it takes. But if, for whatever reason, you fail to complete the course in the three weeks or whatever you have booked, you will have to bear the cost of flying back to America at some future date to complete the course. On which point it is worth noting that to obtain your Temporary Airman Certificate before leaving the USA you must pass the written examinations, whose results can take some time to come through if not taken at an FAA exam centre which uses a computer-based testing system providing 'instant' results. There is also a 30-day wait to re-sit failed parts of the exam, though this can be and often is waived. You must also pass your check ride or practical test (equivalent to the CAA NFT and GFT), after which the Temporary Airman Certificate is issued by the examiner. Without written and check ride passes you will come home with no more than some good flying experience. And since the air fares included in package courses are usually based on non-amendable tickets, you will either have to fly back again at your own expense or stay on and bear the cost of a one-way air ticket to complete the course.

The prospect of learning to fly in clear blue skies, warm sunshine and with sandy beaches nearby may seem attractive, but remember that becoming a pilot — particularly in as short period of time as three or four weeks — will be hard work, and there is unlikely to be much time for anything other than studying, flying, eating and sleeping. Wherever you choose to learn to fly, it should be enjoyable, but do not expect it to be a relaxing holiday.

Another 'overseas' possibility, but much closer to home, is training in the Channel Islands, which are free of VAT and have lower rates of duty on aviation fuel, so it is possible to learn to fly there for less than at some schools on mainland Britain. Operators on Alderney, Guernsey and Jersey (see Appendices) offer residential courses for the CAA PPL and Ratings which include various grades of accommodation as desired. Their PPL courses generally last three/four weeks and include ground school.

Moving up

As we have seen, the Private Pilot's Licence is a minimum qualification. Its scope can be greatly expanded as experience grows by a number of additional 'Ratings' which are briefly described below.

Night Rating

A private pilot who possesses only a basic Private Pilot's Licence cannot legally fly as pilot-in-command after dark when carrying passengers. For post-sunset flight with passengers a Night Rating is required. The minimum experience requirement for application for a Night Rating is 50 hours total flying time of which 25 hours must be as pilot-in-command, with a minimum of five hours' instrument flying instruction. The Night Rating Course consists of a minimum of five hours night flying to include five solo night flights with take-offs and landings, and may be taken before the necessary 50 hours minimum has been achieved (though the rating cannot be granted until the minimum qualifications have been gained), thus making a Night Rating a practical step up to consider shortly after qualifying as a PPL. The Night Rating is non-expiring providing that five solo night circuits and landings have been completed within the six months prior to carrying passengers at night.

IMC Rating

IMC stands for Instrument Meteorological Conditions. As we have seen, the basic PPL restricts the holder to operating within sight of the earth's surface and to a minimum flight visibility of one and a half nautical miles for flight without passengers outside of controlled airspace. Although the PPL syllabus provides a measure of instrument flying instruction aimed at giving a student limited ability to control his aircraft and to perform simple manoeuvres by sole reference to instruments, this is no more than basic insurance against inadvertently entering cloud or poor weather conditions, hopefully enabling the pilot to retain control while returning to a point where visual reference to the ground can be regained. The IMC Rating is the minimum qualification for private pilots seeking to operate in Instrument Meteorological Conditions or under Instrument Flight Rules (IFR), though it does not give *carte blanche* to fly on the Airways system or in controlled airspace, for which a full Instrument Rating (see below) is normally required.

To qualify for an IMC Rating a pilot must have logged a minimum of 25 hours flying in aeroplanes gained after applying for a PPL, of which at least 10 hours must have been as pilot-in-command, including not less than five hours on point-to-point cross-country flights, and must hold a valid R/T Licence.

The IMC Rating course consists of a minimum of 15 hours

dual instrument flying training of which two hours may be conducted on a simulator, and a Ground Training course, followed by a Flight Test and written examination. Again, although the IMC Rating may not be *issued* until the minimum experience qualifications have been met, the flight and ground school courses may be taken in advance, and some students do proceed directly to the IMC Rating course on completion of their PPL training.

The flight training syllabus for the IMC Rating consists of a Basic Stage comprising instrument appreciation and basic and intermediate flight manoeuvres on instruments, together with limited and partial panel flight, and the Applied Stage which covers pre-flight planning, departure and en route flying, instrument let-downs and approaches, and bad weather circuits and landings. PPLs who hold Night Ratings are exempt from three hours of the Basic Stage of the IMC Rating syllabus. The Flight Test, which lasts for approximately one and a half hours, requires the pilot to demonstrate ability to navigate on radio aids while flying solely by reference to instruments, to make a pilot-interpreted instrument approach, and to show ability to use a second type of instrument approach aid, either pilot or ground controller-interpreted. The full syllabus is detailed in *CAP 53*. The IMC Rating is valid for a period of 25 months after a successful flight test, which may be completed in more than one flight, but not more than three. The Ground Training syllabus, for which a minimum of 20 hours' study is recommended, covers physiological factors, aircraft flight instruments, the use of Aeronautical Information Publications, flight planning and the privileges of the IMC Rating. The written examination consists of one paper which includes questions covering the planning and execution of a typical flight under Instrument Flight Rules operating outside controlled airspace. Flight test and written examination must be passed within the six month period preceding an application for an IMC Rating, but there is no specified maximum duration for the course of instruction. A concentrated IMC Rating course should last 6-8 days. The IMC confers only a limited ability to fly in instrument conditions, and is not recognised outside of the UK.

Multi-Engine Rating
In its basic form the Private Pilot Licence covers only Group

A aeroplanes (single-engine landplanes). In order to be able to fly as pilot-in-command of a multi-engined aeroplane a Group B (Multi-Engined aeroplanes with a maximum total weight authorised not exceeding 5700 kilograms) rating is required. Flying multi-engined aeroplanes — in practice this means mostly twin-engined machines in private flying — is not simply a matter of learning how to handle two sets of engine controls and instruments. Multi-engined aircraft are by nature more complex than single-engined machines, generally have higher performance and offer a greater variety of options regarding loading, range and take-off and landing performance than a single-engined aircraft. In particular, the handling and performance characteristics of twin-engined aircraft flying on one engine require training and practice if the advantages of two engines are to be exploited safely.

There is thus a Multi Engine Rating course of a minimum six hours dual flying instruction which is split into two parts: Normal Flight (two and a half hours); and Asymmetric Flight (three and a half hours), and a minimum seven hours of ground instruction followed by flight and oral tests. The flight test includes normal flight procedures applicable to the PPL General Flying Test, plus specific emergency procedures relating to multi-engine aircraft. Once issued the privileges of Group B Rating continue to apply provided that the pilot has flown five hours as pilot-in-command in the previous 13 months (the basic currency requirement for his PPL), though only one flight need have been made in a multi-engine aircraft, and up to two hours of dual instruction may be included in the five-hour total. A Group B Rating may be applied for at the same time as an initial application for a PPL, provided that the required instruction and test have been completed. There have been examples of student pilots completing their entire PPL courses on twin-engined aeroplanes, though few flying schools would be likely to recommend such a course, and the cost would almost certainly be prohibitive.

The Instrument Rating
An Instrument Rating (IR) is the ultimate qualification for a private pilot, though often erroneously regarded as an exclusive preserve of the professional. While it is undeniably

true that qualifying for an Instrument Rating demands no small measure of skill and a great deal of hard work, it is within reach of the dedicated private flier and essential to those seeking to obtain the maximum utilisation from a light aeroplane, since it permits a pilot to operate in controlled airspace under Instrument Flight Rules and thus to use the entire Airways and air traffic control system to best advantage.

Obviously a vital prerequisite to the Instrument Rating (IR) is an ability to fly an aeroplane accurately by sole reference to instruments and to understand and be able to follow air traffic procedures. Before applying to the Civil Aviation Authority for an Instrument Rating a potential candidate must have logged a total of 200 hours of which 100 hours must be as pilot-in-command, at least 35 hours must have been cross-country flying and not less than 40 hours logged as instrument flying. A concession permits half (20 hours) of this latter requirement to have been performed on a simulator. Unless exempt, IR applicants must also complete an approved Instrument Rating course (20 hours dual instruction on single-engined aircraft or 25 hours on multi-engined types) plus 20 hours which may be in an approved simulator, within a 12-month period. Exemptions from these requirements may be granted at the Authority's discretion to military pilots who are instrument-qualified in the Services and in current flying practice; to civilian pilots who have more than 700 hours total flying time of which 200 hours or more are as pilot-in-command; and to holders of IRs for helicopters. Full details of exemptions can be obtained on application to the CAA, who treat each case on its merits. In addition to instrument flight instruction, a minimum of 100 hours ground instruction is required. This may take the form of a course at an approved flying school or a correspondence course (completed in a 12-month period) in preparation for the Instrument Rating written examinations, which are held by the CAA every two months. The examinations comprise six sections: *Flight Rules & Procedures; Flight Planning and Navigation Procedures; Flight Instruments & Radio Aids; Meteorology; Radiotelephony;* and *Signals* with multiple-choice questions on each, and an aural Morse Code Test. A 70 percent pass mark is required in each paper. Failed papers may be re-taken at a later date, but if more than one paper is failed (with the exception of Radiotelephony), all papers must be re-taken. If any single subject is failed twice in succession all papers must also be re-taken and if an applicant fails three attempts there is a mandatory waiting period of three months before a re-sit.

The Instrument Rating Flight Test, which, with the written tests, must be completed within a nine-month period, is conducted by examiners from the Civil Aviation Authority Flying Unit using the applicant's aircraft or one from the school at which he or she has trained.

The Instrument Rating Flight Test consists of an Airways flight using any of a number of standard routes, and typically lasts about two hours. It is divided into four Sections: 1. *Departure procedures;* 2. *Airways procedures;* 3. *Instrument approach procedure;* and 4. *NDB or VOR instrument approach procedure;* and four Sub-sections: A. *Preliminary and external checks;* B. *Holding procedures;* C. *Engine failure procedures;* and D. *Limited panel instrument flying.*

PPL IR applicants must complete all Sections, plus Sub-sections A, B and C. Sub-section C must be completed if the flight test is conducted in a multi-engined aircraft (for which the appropriate Group B rating or other acceptable qualification must be held). The applicant must pass in all Sections and Sub-sections being tested for the award of an Instrument Rating. A partial pass is awarded if any three out of four Sections is passed, but failure in more than one Section means that the entire test syllabus must be taken again. All elements of the IR Flight Test must be successfully completed in a series of three attempts. The maximum number of series permitted also being three (that is, nine attempts overall).

Royal Aero Club FAI Pilot Proficiency Scheme
The Royal Aero Club FAI Pilot Proficiency Scheme was introduced in 1978 as a means of providing proof of a pilot's experience and capability, and to encourage the improvement of private pilots' skills through a series of internationally recognised standards of proficiency. The scheme is entirely voluntary, and although the various proficiency levels are widely recognised, they do not constitute licences or ratings as such.

There are five Proficiency Certificates: Blue; Red; Bronze; Silver; and Gold.

The basic Blue certificate requires a pilot to hold a CAA PPL(A) or equivalent ICAO PPL and a restricted Radiotelephony licence.

The Red certificate requires a minimum of 100 hours total flying time, including at least 40 hours as pilot-in-command, an IMC Rating, one non-stop flight of at least 150 nautical miles, evidence of the study of over-water and mountain-flying techniques, flights from ten different aerodromes including one outside the United Kingdom, and an over-water flight of at least 25 nautical miles.

Both Bronze and Silver certificates require candidates to complete a test paper on radio and general navigation, and meteorology, in addition to greatly expanded experience/ qualification minima.

To qualify for the Gold certificate applicants must possess an Instrument Rating (see alternative below) and a Multi-engine Rating, have a minimum total flying time of 500 hours including 300 hours as pilot-in-command and ten hours of night cross-country flying as pilot-in-command, have made flights from 30 different aerodromes, including five in different foreign countries, and have made at least one flight ranging 750 nautical miles away from departure point.

The following requirements constitute an alternative to an Instrument Rating; — IMC Rating, 1,000 hours total flying, 750 hours pilot in command and 25 hours night flying.

The Royal Aero Club Pilot Proficiency Scheme is open to all United Kingdom licence holders, who can apply to the Scheme headquarters (Robert Pooley, RAeC Pilot Proficiency Scheme, Elstree Aerodrome, Borehamwood, Herts., Tel: 0442 52576) enclosing photocopies of licences and logbook evidence, together with the appropriate application forms. Scroll certificates, ties and lapel badges are available for each level of proficiency, and as proof of achievement a pocket-sized book is issued, endorsed for each certificate obtained.

Any Questions?
To round off this Chapter, here are answers to some common questions which may be in your mind.

I have done some gliding. Will it help with a PPL?
The CAA permit reductions in the minimum hours training requirements for the PPL course for experienced glider pilots, provided that the minimum total of hours of flying experience has been obtained. Holders of Bronze C certificates, or Air Training Corps Instructor ratings, can apply for a PPL subject to having at least 13 hours dual instruction in a powered aircraft, of which at least 10 hours must be as pilot-in-command, including four hours of instrument flying and four hours cross-country flying. Holders of Silver C certificates, or ATC Chief Flying Instructor ratings, or British Gliding Association Instructor ratings, are considered to meet the air experience requirements for a PPL but must show evidence of not less than four hours instrument flying instruction and at least three hours as pilot-in-command within the six months preceding the licence application. No exceptions are made for glider pilots in respect of the mandatory PPL flight test or written examinations, again it is worth emphasising that these are only *minimum* requirements subject to acceptance by the chief flying instructor at your selected school. Some flying schools advise glider pilots to complete the entire PPL course.

Are there any sponsorship schemes?
AERO has provided private flying training and air experience flights for schoolchildren taking GCSE O and A level examinations in Navigation in the past. The Air Education and Recreation Organisation, South West Area Education Office, 14A/B North Street, Guildford, Surrey GU1 4AF. Telephone 0483 572881.

The Air League Educational Trust Flying Scholarships sponsored by the Trust and various industry participants provide up to 15 hours of flying instruction at selected schools to some 20 scholarship winners each year. Open to applicants aged between 18–22 years. Selection by initial application, interview and medical and aptitude tests. Usual closing date for applications 31 July each year. The Secretary, Air League Educational Trust, Grey Tiles, Kingston Hill, Kingston-upon-Thames, Surrey KT2 7LW. (081) 546 9325.

The Fiona McKay Flying Scholarship. To be introduced in 1991 to provide free flying training for young ladies.

Candidates must be UK residents, aged between 18–21. Flying training to be conducted on a vintage Tiger Moth aircraft. Care of the de Havilland Moth Club, Block C, Airfield Estate, Manor Road, Hatfield, Hertfordshire AL10 9LP.

The Geoffrey de Havilland Foundation. Awards flying scholarships of various kinds and as funds permit. British Aerospace, Hatfield Aerodrome, Hatfield, Hertfordshire.

Girls Venture Corps administers the *Hoover Foundation Flying Scholarship.* At least one PPL scholarship awarded each year. Applicants must be GVC members, aged 17–25 years. Selection by senior officer recommendation, written and aptitude tests, interview, trial lesson and test flight. Girls Venture Corps, Redhill Aerodrome, Kings Mill Lane, South Nutfield, Redhill, Surrey RH1 5JY. Telephone 073 782 3345.

International Air Tattoo Flying Scholarships for the Disabled. Awarded in memory of the late Sir Douglas Bader, and partially endowed by King Hussein of Jordan. Provide up to nine totally funded residential PPL courses annually to physically handicapped applicants aged between 18–40 years. Selection by initial application, interview, medical and aptitude tests. IAT Flying Scholarships for the Disabled, Building 1108, RAF Fairford, Gloucestershire GL7 4DL.

Although not a form of flying sponsorship, a number of youngsters have taken jobs with flying clubs and schools under the *Youth Training Scheme* (YTS) and thereby learned to fly and gained their PPLs. Obviously such opportunities are limited, but worth investigating.

I don't want to become a pilot, but I fly as a passenger and would like to learn enough to take over in emergency.
Very wise. What you need is a Second Pilot or 'Pinch Hitter' course, which many flying schools are able to offer. Typically such a course will comprise about 10 hours of dual instruction including some groundschool in basic navigation, meteorology and the use of aircraft radio, and is excellent insurance for regular light aeroplane passengers. Be warned though that you will probably be bitten by the flying bug and want to complete the entire PPL course!

Chapter 3
The Commercial Pilot

As we saw in Chapter 2, the Private Pilot's Licence is strictly an amateur qualification entitling you to fly for personal business or pleasure. To receive payment for your services as a pilot a professional qualification is a legal requirement.

There are in force in the United Kingdom four grades of professional flying licence: Basic Commercial Pilot's Licence (BCPL); Commercial Pilot's Licence (CPL); Senior Commercial Pilot's Licence (SCPL); and Air Transport Pilot's Licence (ATPL), the minimum experience requirements for which are given below, but since requirements and licence privileges can change, readers are advised to consult *CAP 54 — Professional Pilots' Licences* for the latest data on all professional licensing matters.

Basic Commercial Pilot's Licence
Minimum age 18 years. Class I medical certificate (or Class II for pilots not exercising public transport privileges). Approved course of training comprising a minimum of 150 hours of flight training and 400 hours of ground training. Experience requirements for those not taking an approved course are: minimum of 150 flying hours, of which at least 70 hours must be as pilot-in-command, of which 20 hours must be cross-country or over sea flying, and 10 hours of instrument flying instruction. Pilots who cannot meet either the approved course or above requirements but hold a PPL(A) may also qualify for the grant of a BCPL if they have logged a minimum of 200 flying hours, of which 100 hours must be as pilot-in-command, of which 20 hours must be cross-country or over sea flying, and take an abridged course of approved training consisting of 25 hours dual flying

to include training for the IMC rating and BCPL General Flying Test. If an IMC Rating is already held, this is reduced to 15 hours training for the GFT, or 11 hours if a PPL/IR is held.

BCPL (Aeroplanes) applicants must take ground examinations in *Aviation Law, Flight Rules and Procedures; Meteorology; Flight Instruments and Radio Aids; Flight Planning and Navigation Procedures; Signals; Aircraft (General); Aircraft (Type); Performance; Loading; Human Performance and Limitations*; and *Radiotelephony,* and pass a three-part GFT conducted by a CAA Flight Examiner in a single-engined aircraft which comprises tests in cross-country flight, basic aircraft handling and instrument flying (GFTs 1, 2 and 3), and is identical to the GFT for the issue of a Commercial Pilot's Licence (CPL), from which BCPL holders are then usually exempt. Before sitting the BCPL ground examinations candidiates must produce evidence of having completed a course of study given by an 'aeronautical study centre' (not necessarily a flying training school) which is recognised by the CAA. There are a number of these around the country; the CAA can supply a list. BCPL exam candidates must have logged at least 100 hours qualifying flying experience before sitting the examinations. With all professional licensing requirements there are further exemptions for specific cases which are too involved and complex to be dealt with in a book of this kind. *CAP 54 — Professional Pilots' Licences,* or the CAA's Flight Crew Licensing department should always be consulted for specific information.

The BCPL(A) entitles the holder to fly as pilot-in-command or co-pilot of any aeroplane for which the licence holds a valid aircraft rating for any purpose other than public transport. If a BCPL holder has logged 400 hours as pilot-in-command he or she may act as P1 on public transport flights in aircraft weighing less than 2,300 kilograms all-up weight which start and finish at the same aerodrome and do not extend beyond 25 nautical miles (pleasure flying, for example), or as co-pilot on public transport flights in aircraft not exceeding 5,700 kilograms.

Thus, public transport exceptions above aside, the Basic Commercial Pilot's Licence covers what is known as 'Aerial Work' (pleasure flying, glider and banning towing, parachute dropping, for example), and with appropriate ratings also permits the holder to give flying instruction (see below).

Commercial Pilot's Licence

Minimum age 18 years. Must hold Class I medical certificate. Approved course of training of 155 flying hours minimum, of which 100 hours must be as pilot-in-command including 20 hours cross-country, 10 hours night flying, and 10 hours of instrument flying instruction; or, for a combined Commercial Pilot's Licence and Instrument Rating (CPL/IR) an Approved course of 200 hours minimum duration of which 150 hours must be as pilot-in-command, including 50 hours of cross-country flying, 40 hours of instrument flying and 35 hours on multi-engined aeroplanes and about 600 hours of ground school. These minima apply to *ab initio* trainees taking recognised courses approved by the Civil Aviation Authority. Commercial licence applicants who are already experienced pilots may be granted an exemption from taking the course, or part of it, if their total flying experience meets the CAA minimum of 700 hours. All applicants must pass the CPL Technical Examinations which consist of written papers and oral and practical tests in *Aviation Law, Flight Rules and Procedures; Flight Planning; Navigation; Instruments; Meteorology; Radio Aids; Aircraft (General); Aircraft (Type); Performance; Loading; Human Performance and Limitations;* and *Radiotelephony*, and take a General Flight Test which includes demonstrations of the applicant's basic handling, cross-country, and instrument flying, conducted by a CAA Flight Examiner at one of seven regional CAA flight test centres, usually in a single-engined aeroplane. Those applying for a CPL/IR must also undergo an Instrument Rating flight test on a multi-engined aircraft. Holders of BCPLs are usually exempt from certain ground examination subjects if they were passed within the previous five years and are exempt from the CPL GFT.

Senior Commercial Pilot's Licence

Minimum age 21 years. Class I medical certificate. Applicants must have logged a minimum of 900 hours of which not less than 200 hours must be as pilot-in-command (a maximum of 100 hours as a co-pilot performing pilot-in-command duties under supervision is permitted); 50 hours of cross-country or overseas flying of which 35 hours must be as pilot-in-command, including 10 hours which must be at night or on instruments; 25 hours of night flying; and at least 40 hours of instrument flying of which 20 hours may have been logged in a procedures simulator. The balance may be as pilot-in-command, as co-pilot (P2) counted at half-rate, or as bona fide dual instruction. The SCPL is to be phased-out by the middle of this decade; no more are being issued although licences currently held remain valid.

Air Transport Pilot's Licence
Minimum age 21 years. Class I medical certificate. ATPL applicants must have logged 1,500 hours, of which not less than 250 hours must be as pilot-in-command (a maximum of 150 hours as co-pilot performing pilot-in-command duties under supervision is permitted), including at least 200 hours of cross-country flying, 25 hours of which must have been at night; 100 hours of night flying; and 75 hours of instrument flying of which 25 hours may have been logged on a simulator. The remainder may have been logged as pilot-in-command, including up to 400 hours as co-pilot performing pilot-in-command duties under supervision, as co-pilot counted at half-rate, or as bona fide dual instruction.

Commercial Licence holders upgrading to ATPL are not usually required to take another flight test.

Those, in broad terms, are the licensing requirements for UK professional pilots licences. There are thus three principal routes to becoming a professional pilot: the direct route via a purpose-designed BCPL, CPL or CPL/IR course, bypassing the Private Pilot's Licence entirely; or the 'self-improvement' route whereby a Private Pilot can build up the required minimum of 200 or 700 hours towards a BCPL or CPL.

Commercial Pilot Licence Courses
Let us look first at the most direct route: an approved course leading to the issue of a CPL/IR.

There are several Approved flight schools offering CPL/IR courses on fixed-wing aircraft in the United Kingdom, among them Air Service Training at Perth, GB Air Academy at Chichester, the Oxford Air Training School at Kidlington Airport, near Oxford and Trent Air Services at Cranfield Airport.

Ab initio CPL/IR courses last about 13 months and include full ground school, 40 hours of simulator training, and a minimum of 200 hours flying on single- and twin-engined light aircraft. The courses are full-time and (usually) residential. How do you qualify for a CPL/IR course? Schools usually demand minimum educational standards of five passes at GCSE Ordinary Level (or regional or national equivalent), to include English, Mathematics and a Science subject, preferably Physics. These are school requirements and *not* official CAA policy, which lays down no educational standards, though most knowledgeable observers of professional pilot training say that *ab initio* students seeking professional licences should have Advanced Level GCSE passes in Mathematics and Physics or they will find the CPL ground school hard going. It is wise, though not essential, to ensure that you meet the more stringent medical requirements for a Class I Medical Certificate before embarking on a professional licence course. Although a Class III (PPL) medical certificate is adequate for the training period, a Class I certificate must be held before a CPL can be issued, and it is obviously pointless to pursue a training course only to find at the end of it that you are debarred from obtaining your licence for medical reasons. The first medical examination for a professional licence must be conducted by the Civil Aviation Authority Medical Branch's own examiners. Thereafter it can be renewed by Authorised Medical Examiners. The medical standards are higher than those for private pilots, for example impaired hearing or colour blindness, while not necessarily preventing a PPL applicant from obtaining a medical certificate, would likely prohibit the issue of a professional certificate. Renewal intervals for Class I medical certificates are: CPL holders annually up to age 40 years, six-monthly thereafter. SCPL and ATPL holders every six months.

How much does a CPL/IR course cost? At mid-1990 prices a full Commercial Pilot's Licence with Instrument Rating course would cost approximately £45,000–£55,000 inclusive of groundschool, flying, accommodation and VAT. Medical expenses, CAA examination and licence fees and any additional flying training needed beyond the minimum 200-hour requirement will add to that figure.

Not surprisingly, most of the self-financed students at

commercial flying schools come from abroad. The alternative to paying your own way (and incidentally having the money to pay does *not* guarantee a place on a CPL/IR course unless the educational and aptitude requirements are also met), is to find a sponsor. In practice this means an airline, and the question of cadet sponsorships is dealt with in Chapter 4.

Let's pay a visit to a typical commercial pilot training establishment to see just what the CPL/IR course entails. Oxford Air Training School, appropriately located within sight of the spires of the City of Oxford, that traditional seat of learning and scholarship, is one of the world's largest professional flight training establishments.

A substantial proportion of OATS students come from abroad, notably from the Middle East and Africa. For such students their CPL/IR training begins with a 16-week Foundation Course, during which they improve their use of English, especially as related to the technicalities of aviation, and adjust to the foreign environment and living away from home, often for the first time in their lives. The CPL/IR course proper lasts 52 weeks, with two more weeks set aside for vacations, commencing with an initial six-week period of intensive ground instruction. At the end of this groundschool period students take a pre-flight test before proceeding to the next stage; most pass. The failure rate at this point is only one in one hundred. After passing that hurdle the student's working week, Monday to Friday, falls into a routine of integrated Flying/Groundschool, one day in the classroom, one in the cockpit. No part of each 0900–1730 working day is wasted, nor unnecessarily duplicated, for the 52 weeks allocated for the course is little enough. *Ab initio* flying is conducted on Piper Warrior aircraft, whilst advanced work for the Instrument Rating, the final 35 hours of each course, is done on twin-engine Piper Senecas.

Cadets at Oxford live in comfortable motel-style study/bedrooms on the airfield. Unlike university undergraduates they are required to wear the School's blazer-and-slacks uniform during working hours, but otherwise the atmosphere is the comradely, cosmopolitan one of any university, though with longer working hours and perhaps a more purposeful air to the students, who are united by one common aim — to fly *professionally,* in both senses of the word. You might be surprised then to learn that there is a drop-out rate of around 25 percent among CPL/IR trainees. It sounds wasteful, and disappointing for students to work so hard and fail to obtain their licences, but in fact most of the failures occur very early on in the course, usually within the first three months and almost always before the students make their first solo flight. Why? Because the CPL/IR course is intensive from the outset, and failure to cope either in the classroom or in the air quickly manifests itself. The two elements of the course are interdependent; it is no use performing well in the air if ground study lags behind, or vice-versa. One must inevitably have a detrimental effect on the other, and since the time allocated for the course is not overly generous, there is seldom an opportunity for a student who falls seriously behind to catch up.

Students take the Civil Aviation Authority's CPL examinations in the 41st week of their course, but before then they will have taken three internal tests at the School to assess their progress: an Initial Test in Week 13; Interim Test in Week 26; and the Final Test, which determines their suitability for entry for the CPL examinations, in Week 39. Every three months students' progress is monitored by a review board comprising the School Principal, Chief Flying Instructor, Manager of Ground Training and Head of Simulated Flight, who discuss matters with each student informally before preparing a Progress Report, a copy of which is sent to his sponsor. Following the CPL examinations students progress to twin-engined aircraft for the Instrument Rating phase of their training. Simulators play an increasingly important part in professional flight training, particularly for Instrument Flight procedures. They save time and money, and if used as an integral part of a well-planned training syllabus, they permit more effective and economic use of aeroplanes for those parts of the syllabus which can best be taught in the air, such as take-offs and landings, recovery from unusual attitudes or visual cross-country flight. For instrument procedures modern simulators can reproduce virtually everything that might be experienced in a real aeroplane, indeed when converting pilots to new aircraft types in airline service it is now by no means unusual for a trainee to get his or her first 'feel' of the real aeroplane in the air quite late in the conversion course.

Training Concessions for Experienced Pilots

The Civil Aviation Authority grants certain exemptions from the training requirements for Service pilots and for licensed private pilots taking the approved CPL and CPL/IR courses. Pilots qualified and serving with Her Majesty's Forces, and who are *in current military flying practice* with total hours exceeding the minimum licence requirements for the CPL can count their military flight time towards a professional licence. The approved professional flight schools offer ground and flying courses specially tailored for ex-Service personnel seeking to obtain civilian commercial licences. And private pilots who have logged 50 hours or over may be granted a partial exemption from the minimum number of training hours laid down for approved CPL and CPL/IR courses at the discretion of the CAA, but because of the integrated nature of CPL courses, combining ground and flight elements on an alternating basis, such exemptions will probably not reduce the total duration of the course, though they can reduce the overall cost by the number of flying hours credited for PPL experience.

Self-improvement

For those would-be commercial pilots who have no sponsors and cannot afford to pay for an approved course of instruction leading to a CPL or CPL/IR, the so-called 'self-improvement' route is a practical but not easy option.

The key to the self-improvement route lies in finding a way to build flying hours cheaply, free of charge, or best of all be paid for flying, and the most common source of such flying is in training itself. In the past flying instruction could be given by a PPL who had gained an instructor's rating, and was the usual 'ladder' by which the required 700 flying hours needed for exemption from an unabridged CPL course was reached. However, it is no longer legal for PPL-holding instructors to receive payment for instruction. For that the minimum requirement is for an Assistant Flying Instructor (AFI) or Flying Instructor (FI) rating and at least a Restricted Basic Commercial Pilot's Licence. The experience and training requirements for instructor ratings are as follows:

Assistant Flying Instructor

Before starting an approved course of training for the AFI rating, those not already holding professional flying licences

— i.e. candidates for a BCPL(A) — must have logged a minimum of 165 hours total flying experience in aeroplanes, of which not less than 95 hours must have been as pilot-in-command; have passed the GFT; have passed the ground examinations for the BCPL(A); have passed the IMC rating flight test in the preceding 25 months or the Instrument Rating flight test in the preceding 13 months; and hold a Class I or Class II medical certificate. Pre-entry requirements for those already holding a professional licence are: must have logged not less than 100 hours as pilot-in-command of aeroplanes, of which not less than 100 hours must be in single-engined piston-powered types; have not less than 35 hours as pilot-under-instruction; and if less than five hours experience as PIC of single-engined, piston-powered aircraft has been recorded in the preceding 13 months, take a pre-entry flight test.

The approved course for the AFI rating comprises not less than 55 hours ground training and 28 hours flight training, followed by a flight test and oral ground examination by a Flying Instructor Examiner. The basic AFI rating qualifies the assistant flying instructor to give instruction on single-engined aeroplanes up to PPL standard, but not to instruct in applied instrument flying, aerobatics or night flying until additional flight and ground training has been obtained and practical instructional experience has been gained which enables the restriction to be lifted. AFIs may not authorise first solo flights or first solo cross-countries, and may only instruct under supervision of a fully qualified flying instructor.

Flying Instructor
To apply for a Flying Instructor rating applicants must have logged a minimum 400 hours as pilot-in-command of aeroplanes, including not less than 200 instructional hours (or have been an AFI or Qualified Flying Instructor in the UK military forces for not less than six months). A flight test and oral ground examination must also be passed.

Ground studies for the BCPL can take the form of a correspondence course or an intensive (usually residential) course at one of the CAA-approved 'aeronautical study centres'. Assuming you do not intend to remain an AFI throughout your flying career, it makes sense when sitting the BCPL ground examinations to opt instead for the CPL examinations, whose results can be 'banked' for a period of up to five years while you gain the necessary 700 hours needed for the issue of the licence. Even those PPLs who can meet the minimum experience requirements for the issue of a BCPL will also require some flight training to prepare for GFTs 1, 2 and 3. Flying training for the BCPL GFTs is more expensive than for the PPL. Allowing for, say, a minimum of 20 hours' instruction at an average £150 per hour, the cost of exam study courses and CAA flight test and exam fees, a 'self-improver' BCPL is probably going to cost in the region of £4,500, and an AFI course another £3,500–£4,500. One training specialist who has analysed costings estimates the *real* cost of a BCPL with AFI rating at more than £20,000. Factoring in the cost of getting a PPL, hours-building prior to applying for the professional licence, and the likelihood of having to retake parts of the ground examinations and flight tests, with attendant fees each time.

Some large flying schools offer sponsorship schemes whereby selected PPLs have some or all of their AFI course fees paid in return for a peiod of instructing on the staff of the school. The Cabair Group based at Elstree Aerodrome and Oxford Air Training School's General Aviation Centre (see Appendices) are among those which have in the past provided such sponsored training, and can point to a number of former AFIs who have gone on to gain CPLs and ATPLs thanks to this initial 'leg up'.

Another possible source of finance for BCPL or AFI courses is the government-sponsored Career Development Loan scheme, which provides loans of between £300–£5,000 to cover up to 80 per cent of the cost of a vocational training course. Details are available from any JobCentre or from: Freepost Career Development, PO Box 99, Sudbury, Suffolk CO10 6BR.

There are also several competitively-selected annual scholarships for aspiring AFIs:

Amy Johnson Memorial Trust Flying Scholarship: provides financial assistance to a British woman pilot who meets the CAA's AFI experience requirements to gain the AFI rating. Administered by the British Women Pilots' Association.

Norman Motley Scholarship: Provides £1,000 towards the cost of an AFI course. Applicants must meet CAA AFI experience requirements and hold FAI/Royal Aero Club

Bronze Certificate of Proficiency. Applications usually close in the spring. Administered by The Guild of Air Pilots and Air Navigators.

There is no shortage of work for flying instructors, especially during the busy summer months. A full-time Assistant Flying Instructor at a busy flying school should have little difficulty in reaching the 700 hours required for CPL issue within one year. But bear in mind that not everyone is temperamentally suited to becoming an instructor, and the financial rewards are small. It is the most common complaint of flying instructors the world over that they are over-worked and under-paid. The fault lies, to some extent, in the hours-building system. A ready and eager workforce of transient hours-builders, some of whom are happy to work for very low pay in return for free flying time, does little to encourage attractive salaries for instructors, of whom there are increasingly fewer full-time career-orientated people to be found in flying clubs. If, however, you are able to support yourself with another job in spare time, instructing can be the quickest way to accumulate flying time towards a CPL.

The choice between a CPL/IR course and the self-improvement route is really no choice at all. Either you have a sponsor (or the money to pay for the full-time course) or you beaver away accumulating flying hours as fast as you can. Which method produces the best Commercial Pilot? There is a feeling within the professional pilot training industry that a self-improver working up to the 700-hour minimum experience requirement is not so well-equipped for the CPL as the full-time trainee. Certainly a flying diet of five or six hundred hours doing nothing but instructing PPL students or hauling parachutists up to altitude is hardly ideal. But on the other hand, it is arguable that a pilot who can face the hard impecunious path of hours-building from PPL to BCPL to CPL is likely to be better motivated than the sponsored student.

For those who do work their way up, abridged ground-school courses are available at the professional training schools to prepare for the CPL examinations. A typical course lasts eight weeks, timed to finish shortly before the CAA professional licence examinations are held. These courses are usually very well subscribed by 'self-improver'

CPL candidates and are frequently filled a year or more in advance, so early application is advisable.

Training Abroad
There is one further option which might be worth considering for obtaining a Commercial Pilot's Licence. You may have seen in aviation magazines those tempting advertisements from American flight schools which offer *Commercial and Instrument Tickets in Sunny Florida in Only 90 Days!*, usually for amazingly low prices which, allowing extra for return transatlantic air fares and accommodation, promise to reduce the cost of a British CPL/IR course by as much as two-thirds. There has to be a snag, and there is. A US Federal Aviation Administration Commercial Pilot's Licence is not valid for the commercial operation of a British registered aeroplane. In other words, it does not entitle you to earn a living by flying British aircraft in Britain. And unlike the private licence, which can usually be validated locally in foreign countries without too much fuss, there is no reciprocal arrangement whereby an American (or any other foreign) Commercial licence can readily be converted to a British CPL* (see note on page 52). The Civil Aviation Authority would consider time logged on a US Commercial course and make a recommendation for further CPL training accordingly. For the holder of an American Commercial licence who had completed only a basic training course in the United States this recommendation would usually call for around 180 hours further flying training, plus the *full* CPL/IR groundschool course. No shortcut and clearly much more expensive in the final analysis. Passes in FAA ground exams are unlikely to be accepted in lieu of any of the CAA Commercial Pilot's Licence examinations, nor is a GFT exemption likely regardless of experience gained in the USA.

However, if you gain a US Commercial licence and use it to build flying hours cheaply in the United States where aircraft hire rates are much lower than those in Britain, the hours logged — or at least a proportion of them — could be counted towards the minima for a British BCPL or CPL. The CAA's Flight Crew Licensing department assesses such cases individually on merit, so do not believe any claim that a course offered by a US flight school guarantees exemption from British requirements (or a job!) when you get back home.

Many American flight schools offer their successful graduates a job placement service, and US Immigration authorities do permit overseas students to work in the United States for up to 12 months after qualifying provided they have undertaken a career-orientated course of at least six months' duration and the employment is directly related to their field of study, in this case flying. Not all of these 'jobs' are what they seem. Some corporate and third-level aircraft operators who need two-pilot crews to meet operational or insurance regulations use the flight schools as a source of low-paid, or sometimes *un*paid labour. Finding even unpaid flying work in the United States may not be easy, since there are a quarter of a million licensed professional pilots in the country and many tens of thousands of improvers. You would need to have a very special ability to face such local competition.

* A European Commission Directive requires all EC member states to harmonise their professional pilot licensing standards and requirements by 31 December 1992. After that date professional pilots will be trained, tested and examined to a common standard, and licenses issued by one EC state, if all goes according to plan, will be automatically valid in another. At the time of writing, preliminary discussions were under way to determine what the EC licensing requirements will be. The consensus view was that there will be two routes to a Euro CPL — via an* ab initio *'straight through' approved course, and by means of a modular route comprising some approved training and some experience building, as under the UK's present 'self improver' system.*

Helicopters
So far we have been concerned with training on fixed-wing aircraft. However, the increasing importance of helicopters in commercial aviation (in 1968 there were just 136 civil helicopters registered in the United Kingdom; in 1990 there were 861) makes a rotary wing licence a valuable asset for a professional pilot.

The Commercial Pilot's Licence (Helicopters) requirements differ from those for fixed-wing pilots. There is no BCPL of helicopter pilots. The CAA approved course for the CPL(H) calls for a minimum of 150 hours flight training, of which 100 hours must be on helicopters, the remainder may be on aeroplanes, and about 600 hours of ground training. For self-improvers the minimum number of flying hours to qualify for exemption from the approved course is 400 hours on helicopters. The age, medical, ground examination and flight test requirements are the same as for fixed-wing commercial licenses.

Commercial helicopter pilot training courses are offered by a number of operators (see Appendices), but sponsorship is very limited. Of those companies which do have sponsored training opportunities from time to time, perhaps the best-known is Bristow Helicopters at Redhill, Surrey, whose own training school has been operating for more than 30 years. Bristow trains some 30 students each year, mostly to fill first officer positions in its own fleet. Three intakes of students are made each year, comprising a maximum of twelve trainees per course.

Because there is no BCPL and no provision for gaining experience and earning money through flying instruction with a full CPL, the self-improver option is not really viable for helicopter pilots. Operating costs (and therefore the cost of hiring helicopters) are much higher than for aeroplanes, making hours-building towards the minimum 400 hours an expensive business — probably much more expensive than paying for an approved CPL(H) in the first place.

For anyone thinking of a career in civil helicopter flying, an enquiry to the British Helicopter Advisory Board (see Appendices) would probably be as good a starting point as any, and first gaining a PPL(H) would certainly improve the (admittedly limited) chances of sponsorship to a commercial licence.

The Job Market

What kind of employment can a newly-qualified professional pilot expect to be offered? In truth it would be unwise to think of the licence in itself as the key to a wide choice of flying jobs. A freshly-issued licence, with all of 150 or 200 hours logged, is unlikely to bring prospective employers beating a path to your door. Indeed a BCPL or CPL without an Instrument Rating is *very* limiting, since a CPL/IR is mandatory for the commander or co-pilot of any aircraft engaged in scheduled or charter public transport services. A non-instrument rated commercial pilot would thus be limited to a narrow field of activities such as instructing (as we have seen), pleasure-flying, glider-towing, parachute-dropping, perhaps aerial photography of a non-specialised nature, acting as co-pilot on an aircraft not legally required to have two crew or agricultural aviation, though ag flying is a *very* specialised and skilled business and few operators will hire pilots with less than 500 hours experience in agricultural aviation. This 'must have experience' requirement is a common stumbling block for newly-qualified CPLs. How can you gain experience without a flying job, for which you need experience . . . The answer, in most cases, is to swallow pride, pocket your bright new BCPL or CPL and accept employment in some lesser capacity than first pilot in order to gain access to experience building opportunities, and in this respect a pilot who can offer some other skills outside the cockpit (as an engineer, salesman, accountant, office clerk or even van driver, for instance) may well stand a better chance of attracting an employer than one who can fly, full-stop.

The CPL/IR holder is in a stronger position since this licence/rating permits the holder to act as captain of light aeroplanes and to act as co-pilot on *any* aeroplane (though separate Type Ratings are required for operation of aircraft weighing more than 12,500lb). To captain an airliner in commercial service an Air Transport Pilot's Licence is necessary (see the following chapter). Setting aside airline employment which is dealt with below, the opportunities for CPL/IRs in General Aviation are varied. Air-taxi work is an obvious possibility.

Most air taxi operators will require captains to have logged a minimum 1,000 hours flying time, of which 500 must be as pilot-in-command, but co-pilot positions are available to those with less experience. A fixed-base operation which offers flying instruction and ad hoc charter work would also be a good (though not highly-paid) starting point for a new CPL willing to instruct as well as undertake commercial charter flying. Similar openings occur from time to time with operators of private business aircraft.

The commercial pilot job market is cyclical, and at the

Robinson R22 is the most widely-used light helicopter for civilian rotary wing training in Britain, where more than 200 are operating. (Sloane Helicopters)

Simple uncluttered instrument console of the Robinson R22. (Sloane Helicopters)

Aircraft of the British Aerospace Flying College fleet at Prestwick Airport. Top to bottom: Piper Seneca III, Warrior II and FFA Wren. (British Aerospace)

Simulators are a vital part of the airline pilot training and are incredibly realistic. This is British Airways' latest Boeing 747-400 simulator on final approach at the end of a night 'flight'. (Rediffusion Simulation)

The Beech Duchess is typical of light twin-engined aircraft used for multi-engine PPL and CPL training. This one is part of the large training fleet of Wycombe Air Centre in Buckinghamshire. (WAC)

An instrument rating student using a flight simulator for procedures practice, with instructor at left monitoring his progress on a plotter. (Wycombe Air Centre)

Beech Super King Air 350, a typical air taxi and corporate aircraft on which commercial pilots may find positions as co-pilots. (Author)

The Shorts 360 twin-turboprop commuter airliner is widely used throughout the world on 'third-level' routes. (Shorts)

This Gates Learjet 35A operated by Manchester-based Northern Executive Aviation marks the upper end of the air-taxi market. (NEA)

The co-pilot's position on British Airways' large fleet of Boeing 737s will be the first place of work for many of the airline's newly trained pilots. (BA)

The ultimate assignment? British Airways' Concorde. (BA)

Increasing use of helicopters for police surveillance and emergency duties has created new opportunities for experienced ex-military helicopter pilots.

The RAF Air Cadets organisation, which has given thousands of youngsters their first experience of flying, is re-equipping weith these German-built Grob 109B Vigilant motor gliders. (Paul Jackson)

time of writing has been enjoying a boom, but one which is not expected to last, with supply and demand for pilots rapidly reaching equilibrium.

It is clearly impossible in a book of this kind to predict just where employment openings might be at any future time, but aside from the obvious source of vacancies advertised in the aviation press, trade organisations such as the Air Training Association, Aircraft Owners & Pilots Association, British Helicopter Advisory Board, General Aviation Manufacturers & Traders Association and Guild of Air Pilots and Air Navigators or the Student Pilots Association, which is dedicated to assisting those seeking to become professional pilots, (addresses in the Appendices) may be able to offer advice on the current situation.

Chapter 4
The Airline Pilot

In the previous chapter we touched briefly on airline flying from the licensing angle, and with the 'self improver' route to a Commercial Pilot's Licence. Now let us concentrate on the direct route to an airliner's flight deck, through sponsorship by an employing airline, in this case British Airways.

But first, to put the airline employment situation into perspective, it is necessary to go back to the early post-Second World War years of civil aviation in Great Britain. Then, airlines were staffed almost without exception by ex-service pilots, of whom there was a plentiful supply. As air travel burgeoned so the need for a dedicated sponsorship scheme was identified. The two 'flag carriers', British European Airways and British Overseas Airways Corporation (both now merged into British Airways), established the College of Air Training (CAT) at Hamble in Hampshire. There the airlines trained their own sponsored cadets from *ab initio* through to CPL/IR standard, ready to begin type conversion training on the airlines' own fleets. To supplement CAT's output when necessary BEA, BOAC and later British Airways also sent trainees to two private enterprise commercial flying training schools at Oxford and Perth.

The oil crisis of 1973, airline cutbacks and changing demands for travel resulted in a glut of airline pilots as newly-trained personnel joined the many ex-service people who were still flying commercially. When the first edition of this book appeared in 1982 British Airways had some 200 trained cadets who had not been offered employment after graduation from the College of Air Training, which was shortly to be closed for good. Prospects for would-be airline pilots were depressingly poor.

And yet, there were those in the industry who (quite correctly as it has transpired) predicted a complete reversal, anticipating a retirement 'bulge' in the mid-1980s as those young pilots who had joined the airlines in the early 1950s reached mandatory retirement age. And so, in February 1987 the British national airline began advertising for applicants to sponsor for training as commercial pilots. Within four weeks of the first advertisement appearing the company had received 3,500 enquiries, and that was rather fewer than it had expected.

British Airways' studies of its pilot recruitment and training policies, based on anticipated aircraft fleet numbers, estimated flying hours and thus crew required, suggest that the airline will need to recruit between 100–160 new pilots each year, of which it plans to supply 85 per cent from sponsored trainees, making up the balance from direct-entry qualified pilots.

British Airways defined its requirements for sponsored trainees by drawing up a specification based on a profile of its existing pilot workforce. A cross-section of captains and first officers were invited to define the qualities they considered important for doing their jobs, and to act as guinea pigs in taking aptitude and selection tests that were being developed for the new crop of recruits. Teams from polytechnics and sixth form colleges were also invited to take the tests in order to assess how differing backgrounds, working environments and 'life experiences' reflected in the performance of 'candidates'.

Let us look then at the resulting British Airways' cadet selection process. The basic requirements are straightforward: you must be a British subject with a right to residence; male or female (about one in 16 cadets are women), with the right to a worldwide, unrestricted British passport; age over 18 and under 24 years by 31 December of the year of application; height between 1.63 and 1.93 metres; and possess a minimum of five passes in GCSE Ordinary level examinations, including English Language, Mathematics and a Science subject, and two passes at Advanced level, ideally Maths and Physics, or three Scottish Highers, or two Irish Leaving Certificates — honours at 'C' grade or above. Those sitting GCSE 'A' levels in the year of application are also eligible.

Successful applicants are likely to have three 'A' level passes and eight or more passes at 'O' level. Science orientation is all but mandatory. Twenty years ago 'A' level passes in Arts subjects would have stood an applicant a reasonable chance of being accepted for the selection process at least, but experience has shown that many Arts-orientated cadets found difficulty in coping with groundschool training and suffered higher failure rates than their Sciences-based colleagues. Because of schools' tendency to 'stream' students into Arts or Sciences disciplines after GCSE Ordinary level examinations, anyone hoping for a BA cadetship thus needs to be thinking of subject specialisation before taking 'O' levels, which means at the age of 14–15 years, since Sixth Form streaming usually reflects performance in 'O' level examinations. Such is the intensity of competition that an Arts qualified school leaver is likely to be at a disadvantage.

It is worth stating here that this 'sciences only' emphasis is not universally shared in the airline pilot training industry. Some experienced training staff feel that the case for Mathematics and Physics is over-stated and that a good rounded education, perhaps with subjects such as Economics at 'A' level, produces equally suitable airline captain material. However, if the sponsoring airline wants a Sciences person, so be it.

On the subject of graduate trainees there is more agreement. A university degree is by no means essential for professional pilot training courses. Most cadets recruited by sponsoring airlines in Britain have *not* been to university. A degree could even be a career hindrance. Because of the age limits set on potential recruits, a graduate is likely to be leaving university at the same age as a direct-entry school-leaver would be starting route flying after completing training.

The 'winnowing' process begins on receipt of an initial enquiry. Selection then proceeds (as a rough benchmark) on a 'ten per cent' basis. That is to say, if 15,000 enquiries are received, 1,500 will probably be suitable for further selection procedures, and of those 150 may prove eligible for sponsorship, of whom (as a 'worst case' average) 15 might be expected to drop out during flying training. The GCSE standards alone narrow the potential 'catchment area' to the top few per cent of the educational spectrum, so anyone who can meet the airline's exacting selection requirements will be a very high calibre individual who could go to university or into almost any of the professions.

So, after initial enquiries, those who appear appropriately qualified are invited to make formal application. There are two application forms. One requests details of educational accomplishments, school, college or university activities, social and sporting interests, previous employment if any, aviation experience, and 'career objectives': why do you want to be an airline pilot?; what attracts you to British Airways?; what have you done with your life that might help you as a pilot; what is your expectation of a career as an airline pilot?

The second form is a biographical questionnaire which contains 52 probing questions with multiple choice answers, for example: what kind of holidays do you prefer?; do you enjoy meeting new people?; how successful do you rate yourself to date?; how often do you tell other people your troubles?

Are there are particular attributes which the airline looks for in a prospective cadet? Yes. First, be as close to 18 years of age as possible; 'catchy youngy, teachy easy' is the byword. Secondly, a *genuine* interest in flying, to which end the biographical questionnaire asks a number of questions about the applicant's interest in aviation, such as when it first arose, whether he or she ever visits air displays or aviation museums, or subscribes to aeronautical magazines.

Very important is a record of previous solo powered flight experience, not because of any possible reduction in training hours (it makes no difference), but because it proves that applicants can actually *fly* an aeroplane, that they like it, and that they want to do more of it. The airline has found that dual flying experience or gliding is no real advantage, indeed candidates with only dual experience fared rather worse than those totally without flying experience; having managed the engine of a powered aircraft as well as the flying controls is a good test of coordination. All other things being equal, a PPL or at least solo flight logged, Air Training Corps or Combined Cadet Corps experience, a RAF Flying Scholarship or, for university graduates, flying experience with a University Air Squadron would all be good things to have on your record. As a BA flight crew recruitment manager put it: "Those with an abiding love of aeroplanes and flying make the happiest employees in our experience. If they can just get their hands on something that flies . . . If not, aeromodelling would be a good start."

What then of those who select a career in airline flying as one of several possible options carrying a high salary? In the past British Airways did employ some people who simply drew up a short list of desirable jobs, but the airline believes current selection processes will weed those out.

The age at which academic qualifications are attained is significant, GCSE passes achieved first time, with no resits would be a plus, and an academic course leading to passes in Maths and Physics at 'A' level is, if not vital, then very desirable. It is also important to develop social skills and to have taken an active part in group activities and taken responsibilities.

All pilots and trainees are selected on the assumption that they will become captains. The days when airline captains were aloof from the remainder of the crew are long gone. They are now more than ever a part of a team, and the airline looks for people who can get along with their colleagues, both on the flight deck and in the cabin, and with the passengers, and who will be sufficiently self confident and assertive not to hesititate to question an action on the flight deck if the need arises: high achievers, strong socially confident leaders possessing team skills.

Some of this can be gleaned from answers on the application forms, but the sorting process begins in earnest on primary assessment. Shortlisted applicants are invited to undertake initial written aptitude and ability tests which probe mental agility, critical thinking, mechanical reasoning and technical numeracy at British Airways Recruitment and Selection Centres around the country. The second stage involves a one-day visit to British Airways' Meadowbank Recruitment and Assessment Centre at Heathrow Airport, where candidates are tested eighteen at a time in two batches of nine each in a computerised testing facility — the first of its kind to be installed by a European airline. The tasks comprise a series of computer-based tests to determine hand-eye coordination, tracking control, the ability to interpret instruments, spatial awareness, and basic motor activity. The Meadowbank facility has nine testing stations, each with a computer, VDU and miniature set of aircraft 'controls', all linked to a master instructor's console. Candidates' scores are automatically computed and printed out, to be normed against averages established in the tests on BA's existing workforce. The anticipated pass rate at this stage is in the order of one in every three or four. Those who are successful at this stage are asked to complete a medical questionnaire and to have a medical examination (not an aviation medical) performed by their own doctor, at the airline's expense.

Then it is back to Meadowbank in groups of five for a two-day assessment phase, which comprises written tests, assessment of team skills and 'personality profiling'. Discussion subjects are set, with candidates nominated to lead, sum up and report, ensuring that everyone gets a fair chance. Group exercises, called structured leadership tests, are also employed. The candidates are set a problem which has a finite solution and they have to find it and prepare a written report, but BA does not go in for those "here's a plank of wood and an old tyre, now cross this shark infested river" types of exercise. Candidates are then individually assessed at two interview sessions with the Pilot Board and the Personnel (Human Resources) Board, each made up of two people.

Once over those not inconsiderable hurdles the final phase is to attend the CAA Medical Branch for a full Class I medical examination by CAA and British Airways medical staff. Historically there has been a five per cent failure rate at this final stage. The disqualifying medical problems have no particular pattern, but colour blindness and childhood illnesses which have left hitherto undetected weaknesses are among them. The fit can expect to receive a formal offer of sponsorship and a place on a future training course.

What British Airways actually offers to those successful applicants is a loan covering the total cost of flying and ground training, equipment, accommodation and food. For this reason trainees must be aged 18 years at the time of accepting an offer so that they may legally sign the loan form. If, at the end of training, the airline offers them a job, the loan is written off providing the newly qualified pilot contracts to stay with British Airways for five years. If no job is forthcoming (at the best of times prospects for pilots employment are ever a case of feast or famine) there is no obligation to repay if no post has been offered within a year of completion of the training course. Should a trained cadet decline a co-pilot position with the airline, the full amount (around £60,000 at current estimates) is repayable.

Where do candidates go for training? To Prestwick Airport, where British Aerospace began training the first BA-sponsored pilots in January 1988 at the newly-established Flying College, which at the time of writing in late 1990 plans to take 160 BA cadets each year.

The course at Prestwick lasts 16 months, and begins with eight weeks of ground tuition. Modern facilities at the Flying College include classrooms equipped with push-button answering systems linked to a 'tell tale' panel monitored by the tutor, so that when questions are asked he can tell at a glance if an incorrect response has been given.

Flying training commences with a 55-hour course on Piper Warrior aircraft which is devoted principally to basic handling. Cadets then move on to the Swiss-built FFA Bravo, which is known as the Wren on the College fleet. the Wren is fully aerobatic and cleared for spinning, so is used to introduce trainees to more advanced flying techniques, and also to solo cross-country work; 40 hours are flown on Wrens, together with a further 60 hours of instrument training on Warriors, bringing total single-engine experience to 155 hours. This is followed by a 45-hour multi-engine course on Piper Seneca IIIs. Part of the multi-engine training is crew-orientated 'mutual' flying with two trainees sharing cockpit duties. The aircraft are equipped with instrument panels which duplicate as far as possible the standard flight deck arrangement adopted in the airline's fleet, and dedicated simulators for each type are installed at Prestwick. Some 40 hours simulator flying are included in the course, at the end of which trainees spend a further sixty hours in jet simulators — a BAe 125/700, or for those destined for airliners equipped with CRT-based electronic flight instrument systems (EFIS, or so-called 'glass cockpits'), a BAe 125/800.

This phase of training is known as LOFT (Line Orientated Flying Training). Its purpose is fourfold. First, to introduce cadets to company procedures. They 'fly' standard British Airways schedules, which sometimes mean getting calls to report for duty in the small hours, just as operational crews do, and are expected to act in every respect as line pilots. The Flying College at Prestwick has direct links with BA's computerised flight planning and meteorological facilities at Heathrow, so that on every 'flight' trainees get used to doing things 'the British Airways way'. The aim is for 'seamless' training, so that by the time newly qualified cadets come to the airline's simulator centre at Cranebank near Heathrow for type conversion training, company procedures will be entirely familiar. Secondly, LOFT provides an introduction to the higher speeds at which everything happens when flying jets. Thirdly, it teaches cadets to function as a crew; and finally it provides an opportunity for airline staff to assess the students as future captain and first officer material.

The airline is dedicated to the two-crew concept, and although British Airways' fleet will not become all two-pilot until well into the first decade of the 21st century (some older Boeing 747s, TriStars and the Concordes are expected to be operational at least until 2007), the rank of second officer has already disappeared: all new pilots become first officers on joining the airline now, and on check-out immediately fly as second-in-command.

While at the BAe Flying College trainees must wear full BA uniform, but without rank markings. They are accommodated and fed free of charge in a hall of residence that was formerly a hotel, and paid weekly 'spending money'. Resident BA first officers provide a link between the trainees and the organisation for which they will be working and act as 'role models'.

The course lasts 70 weeks, after which graduates emerge with a CPL/IR and a 'frozen ATPL' (they will have passed the ATPL exams, but need to accumulate flying hours to reach the ATPL minima). The failure rate recorded in the first three years of training is a remarkably low three and a half per cent (the airline had deemed ten per cent acceptable, if failures occurred in the first 25 hours before too much time and money had been spent on the failed trainee). Those who fail to complete the course mostly do so because of academic shortcomings or for disciplinary reasons rather than lack of flying ability.

Operational training following the BAe Flying College

course begins with a familiarisation stage when new recruits get acquainted with the many facets of running an airline beyond the flight deck: traffic management, engineering, ticket sales, even catering.

Once the introductory get-to-know-your-airline phase is over, work begins on training for a Type Rating on the multi-engine jet types which the new pilots will fly operationally. For a newly trained ex-cadet this would normally be one of BA's short range aircraft such as the BAC 1-11 or Boeing 737, which they will fly exclusively until 'converted' to another type later in their careers. As a rule pilots do not fly more than one aircraft type during any one phase of their careers, though they may hold type ratings for several.

Training for the type rating is conducted at Cranebank, where BA has the latest audio-visual training aids, cockpit procedures trainers and full-motion computer-generated-image flight simulators for all aircraft in its fleet except Concorde, the simulator for the supersonic aircraft being owned by co-manufacturer British Aerospace at its Bristol-Filton facility. British Airways has Civil Aviation Authority approval for Level 4 'zero flight time' type ratings on several of its simulators, which means that pilots can be type-rated on the aircraft solely on simulator practice, and may fly the actual aircraft for the first time on a scheduled service.

After a three-month conversion course at Cranebank new pilots are released to the line as co-pilots under supervision, in which role they must fly a minimum of 70 sectors and pass route checks before being cleared as fully qualified co-pilots. From start of training to operational flying takes slightly less than two years.

The first opportunity to change aircraft type is likely to occur after some five years of line flying. Pilots can 'bid' for crew vacancies on other aircraft fleets — moving up to larger short haul aircraft such as the Boeing 757, 767 or the long haul Lockheed TriStar and Boeing 747. If successful they would undergo further conversion training to gain the new type rating.

It is reasonable to assume that everyone who embarks on a career as an airline pilot eventually seeks the coveted left hand seat of an airliner, the captain's position. Equally, when selecting recruits and throughout the continual training process which is part of every airline pilot's life, the airlines view every pilot as a potential future captain. They do not mark certain trainees as lifetime co-pilots and others as captains; in theory everyone selected has the stuff of command within, but obviously not everyone can achieve the ultimate ambition.

The command structure is based on seniority, but becoming a captain is not automatic. British Airways regards the mid-point of a pilot's career as the appropriate time to consider promotion to captain on short-range aircraft. As a probationary captain a pilot would have to demonstrate to a training captain the ability to make sound, commercially viable, operationally safe decisions and to be able to direct and coordinate the work of flight crew, cabin crew and ground staff over a large number of flights before being granted full command. After three to five years in command an opportunity might then arise to switch aircraft types.

The ideal career structure in the airline's view is to fly as co-pilot on two or three types of aircraft, then, following a mid-career promotion to captain, follow the same pattern in command.

Other sponsors

Apart from British Airways, several other British airlines offer (or have in the past offered) sponsorship schemes, although the cyclical nature of the airline pilot job market makes it impossible to predict when trainees may be recruited.

British Midland Airways and Britannia Airways operate Bursary Sponsorship schemes in conjunction with the Oxford Air Training School which involve the trainee paying part of the cost (around 50 per cent in two parts, some of which may be deducted in instalments from eventual salary) of training to CPL/IR standard, with the airline paying the balance and offering a five-year contracted flight deck position once qualified. Age limits are 18–26, with much the same educational and other selection criteria as applied by British Airways, and courses are run twice a year. Details of these schemes may be obtained from: Bursary Selection Office, Oxford Air Training School, Oxford Airport, Kidlington OX5 1RA.

Another possibility, though more suited to 'self-improvers', is the Joint Sponsorship Scheme operated by the Cabair group of companies in conjunction with Air UK and Britannia Airways. It is open to those aged 18–31 who hold a Private Pilot's Licence with IMC Rating and 150 flying hours logged. Selected applicants pay around £4,000–£5,000 towards the cost of getting a basic Commercial Pilot's Licence, after which they work for about two years as flying instructors with the Cabair group's flying schools before joining the co-sponsoring airline as first officers, with some 1,000 flying hours logged and two years aviation work experience behind them.

Apart from direct sponsorship schemes such as those outlined, where else do airlines recruit pilots? There are two principal sources: from a pool of Commercially-licensed pilots working for other airlines or in other branches of civil aviation such as flying instruction and air taxi work; and from the armed services.

What are the chances of a 'self-improver' Commercial pilot getting an airline job? It depends naturally on the state of the job market at the time, but in recent years the 'retirement bulge' and growth in regional air services and 'third level' carriers, often operating relatively unsophisticated twin turboprop aircraft, have increased opportunities for employment, and sharply increased the demand for commercial pilot training courses.

Examples of successful self-improvers who have reached airliner flight decks are not hard to find. One woman pilot interviewed by the author was flying as a first officer three years after taking a trial flying lesson. She managed to borrow the cost of a Private Pilot Licence course (but only after applying to several bank managers who considered her ambition to become a professional pilot unrealistic), completed the course in a month and worked a further six months in a non-flying job to pay off the debt. Another period of employment with an aviation company earned a modest salary but included about two hours free flying each week, and with more help from an understanding bank manager she took an Instructor's Rating course which enabled her to build hours towards a Commercial Pilot's Licence and Instrument Rating. Three years after first handling an aircraft's controls she was co-piloting a Shorts 330 commuter airliner.

Her story is by no means unique, but it is worth noting

that apart from a mandatory CPL/IR, the minimum experience level which any airline will normally set before considering a pilot is 1,000 hours, subject of course to successfully meeting other criteria (motivation, character, performance, medical and psychological suitability) as applied to *ab initio* recruits. One common thread which runs through every success story of self-improvers attaining an airline position is dedication to achieving that goal. There are no guarantees, no shortcuts. The route is long, arduous, expensive in time and money, often dispiriting, but for those who make it — and it has to be said that many do not — ultimately very rewarding.

Chapter 5
The Military Pilot

A career with the Armed Services offers some of the finest pilot training and certainly the most exciting flying in the world.

Competition for a trainee pilot's position is thus extremely fierce, and the selection procedures rigorous, with good cause, for the cost of training a RAF fast jet pilot to squadron service standard is in excess of £3 million. Small wonder then that for every 200 enquiries received from aspiring service pilots, on average only one will successfully negotiate the selection and training procedures described below to become a RAF pilot.

The Royal Air Force recruits aircrew officers either directly (from school, polytechnic, university or civilian life) or via a RAF-sponsored University Cadetship scheme. A major change in recruitment policy was announced in July 1989 when, for the first time since its formation in 1918, women became eligible to serve as RAF pilots and navigators, following a study which recommended broadening the opportunities from women in the Service. Women pilots, the first of whom commenced training in early 1990, will not fly fast jets or combat helicopters, but will be permitted to fly transports, tankers, airborne early warning and search-and-rescue aircraft and to serve as flying instructors. Target recruitment is for an annual total of 270 RAF pilots, of whom up to ten per cent may be women.

The Royal Air Force

The minimum age and educational requirements for RAF aircrew entrants are as follows: School-leavers, Graduates, Civilians: Age 17½-24 years on entry, though application must be made before reaching the age of 23½ years; at least five passes at GCSE Ordinary Level at Grade C or above, including English Language, Mathematics and a relevant science subject, or a University degree in any subject. Applicants must be subjects or Citizens of Great Britain or the Republic of Ireland; or have been born in a country which is (or then was) within the British Commonwealth or Republic of Ireland; or have both parents who meet (or met) those qualifications. In exceptional circumstances a dispensation against these requirements may be made at the discretion of the Secretary of State for Defence, but all applicants must possess British nationality at the time of application, and applicants not of United Kingdom origin must normally have been resident in the United Kingdom for a minimum period of five years.

University Sponsorship. As part of the Royal Air Force's Graduate Entry Scheme sponsorships are available to undergraduates and prospective undergraduates taking full-time degree courses at a recognised UK educational establishment. RAF University Cadetship awards lead to Permanent Commissions in the service and attract a starting salary of some £11,000 per year. In addition, university fees are paid by the RAF. Bursary awards are also available, but without fees payment or prejudice to local education authority grants, and lead to Short Service Commissions.

University Air Squadrons

Before moving on to examine the selection and training procedures for the Royal Air Force, it is worth looking at the role of the University Air Squadrons (UASs). Lord Trenchard conceived the idea of forming Air Squadrons at Oxford and Cambridge Universities in 1919, with the declared object of 'encouraging an interest in flying, and promoting and maintaining liaison with universities in technical and research problems affecting aviation . . . (and) to assist those who wished to take up aeronautics as a profession, either in the Royal Air Force or in a civilian capacity, and those who, whilst not making aviation their career, desired to give part-time service to defence in the non-regular air force.'

That is precisely the function of the 17 UASs (see list below) which exist today under direct command of RAF

Support Command from Headquarters University Air Squadrons at RAF College, Cranwell in Lincolnshire. The UASs form the largest flying training organisation within the RAF, and are affiliated to 56 universities, university colleges and polytechnics throughout the British Isles.

There are three classes of University Air Squadron membership: RAF Volunteer Reserve members, Bursars and University Cadets. RAF Volunteer Reservists are university undergraduates who want to learn to fly but may not wish to enter the RAF for a career, and are not committed to doing so. Recruitment is usually carried out within the first week of a new university year, and applications exceed available places by a factor of four or five to one. Women undergraduates were permitted to join UASs from 1985, and now comprise some ten per cent of total UAS strength nationwide. RAF(VR) members are enlisted as Aircraftsmen (or women) but enjoy the status of Officer Cadets. Whilst not having to undergo the rigorous aptitude tests which RAF aircrew entrants must take, RAF(VR) members must pass medical and selection boards before flying service aircraft. RAF(VR) membership of UASs is limited to a duration of two calendar years, but may be extended for a further year to those seriously interested in pursuing a flying career with the RAF.

Bursar and University Cadet UAS members are sponsored by the RAF following acceptance by the Officer and Aircrew Selection Centre, currently at RAF Biggin Hill but planned to move to RAF College Cranwell. Bursars are committed to Short Service Commissions with the RAF after university graduation. University Cadets are commissioned and paid as Acting Pilot Officers while studying, and after graduation enter the service as junior officers. All RAF-sponsored university undergraduates, including those destined for careers in the ground branches of the service, automatically become UAS members.

In a typical UAS, RAF(VR) members outnumber Bursars and University Cadets about to two one. The number of University Cadets within the total UAS flying membership (which typically numbers around 950–980) must not exceed 30 per cent overall (50 per cent of any one squadron) in order to preserve the relationship between each educational establishment and its squadron (and, one imagines, to assuage fears that UASs are merely recruiting gimmicks, which they certainly are not). Individual squadron membership varies between 40–80 according to the number and size of educational establishments served, and the geographic spread of UASs and detachments is such that few major educational centres are denied access to a squadron within an acceptable travelling distance.

There are two UAS flying training courses: the Basic Course provides for 20 hours training per year over two years, while the Long Course, open to especially able undergraduates and all RAF-sponsored pilot University Cadets, provides for 33 hours per year over three years. For RAF(VR) members completing the Basic Course, 40 hours training is often sufficient to qualify them for a civilian Private Pilots Licence after taking the relevant CAA examinations and flight tests without completing a civilian PPL course, although this is not one of the aims of UAS membership, and issue of a civilian licence is at the discretion of the Civil Aviation Authority.

UAS flying courses are conducted on a fleet of 80 Scottish Aviation Bulldog T.1 two-seat trainers. The Basic Course syllabus comprises general handling and circuit procedures leading to first solo (usually after 11 hours dual instruction), instrument training and navigation. Students' progress is closely monitored and tested at 'critical points', each of which must be passed satisfactorily before moving on to the next stage of training. After 35–40 hours students must take a Basic Handling Test (BHT), which equates approximately to the experience level required for a civilian PPL and should be within reach of all UAS students. The much-prized RAF Preliminary Flying Badge (PFB) requires a minimum of 65 hours flying, and is typically awarded at 70–80 hours, and is thus generally only achievable by Long Course students or university-sponsored students staying in the UAS for a third year's flying. Long Course students, who include all University Cadets destined for pilot careers in the service, also learn instrument flying procedures, aerobatics and formation flying, bringing them up to Cranwell Entry Standard (CES) and enabling them to qualify for shortened basic flying training courses at Flying Training School or the RAF College Cranwell. Some forty to fifty per cent of all pilots joining the RAF's fast-jet squadrons come from a UAS background.

The UASs are not just a good source of free flying for university students. Military discipline has to be observed, uniform worn, and a substantial commitment of time demanded, typically one or two half-days each week during term time for flying training, and one evening per week for ground studies, although care is taken to ensure that over-enthusiastic pilots do not neglect their academic studies in favour of flying! During the university or polytechnic summer vacations UASs deploy to RAF stations for a four-week summer camp devoted to concentrated flying and gaining an insight into service life, often helping in the day-to-day working of the station. In addition there is a wide range of sporting and social activities and inter-squadron competitions to be enjoyed.

The following University Air Squadrons are currently active:

Squadron	Academic Institutions served	Base
Aberdeen, Dundee and St. Andrews UAS	Aberdeen University, Dundee University, Dundee Institute of Technology, Robert Gordon Institute of Technology, St. Andrews University	RAF Leuchars
University of Birmingham UAS	Aston University, Birmingham Polytechnic, Coventry Polytechnic, Birmingham University, Keele University, Staffordshire Polytechnic, Warwick University, Wolverhampton Polytechnic	RAF Cosford
Bristol UAS	Bath University, Bristol Polytechnic, Bristol University, Exeter University	Bristol-Filton Aerodrome
Cambridge UAS	Cambridge University	Cambridge Airport
East Lowlands UAS	Edinburgh University, Heriot-Watt University, Napier College of Commerce & Technology, Stirling University	RAF Turnhouse

East Midlands UAS	Nottingham University, Leicester University, Leicester Polytechnic, Loughborough University of Technology, Trent Polytechnic	RAF Newton
Glasgow and Strathclyde UAS	Glasgow University, Glasgow College of Technology, Strathclyde University, Paisley College of Technology	Glasgow Airport
Liverpool UAS	Liverpool University, Lancaster University, Liverpool Polytechnic, Lancaster Polytechnic	RAF Woodvale
University of London UAS	London University, City University, Brunel University	RAF Abingdon

Manchester and
  Salford UAS
	Manchester University,
	Salford University,
	University of Manchester Institute
	  of Science & Technology,
	Manchester Polytechnic
		RAF Woodvale

Northumbrian UAS	Durham University, Newcastle University, Newcastle Polytechnic, Sunderland Polytechnic, Teesside Polytechnic	RAF Leeming
Oxford UAS	Oxford University, Oxford Polytechnic	RAF Abingdon

Queens UAS	Queens University Belfast,
	University of Ulster, Coleraine
	  and Jordanstown
		Belfast (Sydenham)
		  Airport

Southampton UAS	Southampton University, Portsmouth Polytechnic	RNAS Lee-on-Solent

University of Wales
  UAS
	University College of Wales,
	  Aberystwyth,
	University College of North Wales,
	University of Wales College
	  of Cardiff,
	University College of Swansea,
	University of Wales College
	  of Medicine,
	St David's University College
	  Lampeter,
	The Polytechnic of Wales
		RAF St. Athan

Yorkshire UAS	Bradford University, Hull University, Leeds University, Sheffield University, York University Sheffield Polytechnic, Leeds Polytechnic, Huddersfield Polytechnic	RAF Finningley

73

Selecting Aircrew for the Royal Air Force

Direct Entrants and University Cadets both begin their RAF careers with an application to the Officer and Aircrew Selection Centre (OASC) currently at the former Battle of Britain fighter station at RAF Biggin Hill in Kent, but due to be relocated to RAF College Cranwell in 1992. Application is made on a six-part buff form RAF Form 6520, which has sections for *Personal, Educational, Previous Employment, Recreation, Previous Military Service, Flying Experience* and *General* information.

Selection of potential aircrew is carried out by either The Air Board (Direct Entrants) or The Cadetship Board (candidates for RAF-sponsored University Cadetships). The two-part selection process at Biggin Hill takes three days for Direct Entrant aircrew applicants and four days for would-be University Cadets. Applicants arrive at Biggin Hill either on a Saturday or on a Monday. Their first day at the OASC is devoted to getting to know fellow candidates and undergoing a chest X-ray. On the second day candidates take aptitude tests aimed at finding out how each will respond to aircrew training, measuring their ability to *learn* rather than their ability to perform at this stage.

The OASC uses computer-based aptitude tests for prospective aircrew in place of earlier electro-mechanical devices. Fifty-three individual computer monitors/keyboard stations are used to test applicants for all the British services and some overseas forces, with an annual throughput of 8,000 potential pilots, navigators and controllers.

The computer equipment analyses a candidate's co-ordination of hand, eye and foot; rate control; instrument interpretation; spatial awareness; memory, deductive reasoning; selective attention; information scheduling and perceptual speed, all of which are valuable pointers to his ability to fly, navigate and fight with a modern jet aircraft. After some 11 tests have been completed the computer provides examiners with an instant analysis which enables them to determine a candidate's suitability for further testing as a possible pilot (or navigator or controller) trainee. On the third day candidates undergo a thorough medical examination. To avoid disappointment at this stage through failing the medical, candidates aged between 16-16½ years can take a RAF Medical Board examination and the aptitude tests before applying for entry into the service. Successful completion of the tests does not however guarantee future selection, nor does it place the examinee under any obligation to join the RAF later.

After the medical examination there is a 40-minute character assessment interview conducted by two RAF officers, followed by 'syndicate tests'. Each 'syndicate' consists of a team of five or six candidates who are supplied with numbered overall suits to preserve their anonymity. The syndicate meets with a board of interviewing officers who offer subjects for discussion, the idea being that the subsequent conversations will reveal how each applicant responds to others, whether he or she mixes easily or is reticent, whether he is a leader or a follower. Next the syndicate is set a planning exercise in which a specific task is outlined and the candidates must draw up a plan of action and justify their decisions. The final round of team tests consists of a practical exercise (for example, crossing a hangar floor without touching the ground using only a couple of planks and some suspended motor tyres), which looks like a practice session for the Royal Tournament but is aimed at assessing qualities of leadership, courage, judgement, enthusiasm, initiative and determination.

Those who complete the Selection Course satisfactorily can usually expect to hear whether or not they have been accepted for aircrew entry or a university cadetship within a month of their visit to the Officer and Aircrew Selection Centre. Rejected applicants may re-apply for further assessment at the OASC provided they have not exceeded the maximum age limits for entry. In practice the RAF recommends a wait of two years before re-applying, although those aged under 21 years may re-apply after a wait of at least 12 months. Those who fail the flying aptitude tests may be invited to complete further selection tests for non-aircrew careers if they have opted for alternative choices on their initial applications.

Aircrew Training

Once selected, new aircrew recruits for the RAF undergo an 18-week Initial Officer Training (IOT) course at RAF Henlow near Bedford (direct entrants from school or civilian life) or the RAF College at Cranwell in Lincolnshire (graduates). The IOT course prepares entrants for their responsibilities as junior RAF officers. It includes drill routine, assault courses, initiative tests, survival training and general physical activities such as canoeing and mountain climbing.

After IOT, direct entrants with no previous flying experience undergo 63 hours basic training in de Havilland Chipmunk training aircraft at the Elementary Flying Training School, RAF Swinderby.

At present RAF *ab initio* flying training — apart from that conducted at University Air Squadrons and the Flying Selection Squadron — is performed on the Shorts Tucano T.Mk 1 turboprop and the aircraft which it is gradually replacing, the venerable Jet Provost T.5

Direct entrant Basic Flying Training courses are conducted at No 1 Flying Training School, RAF Linton-on-Ouse or No 7 Flying Training School, RAF Church Fenton. The 37-week course consists of 93 flying hours. Graduates with UAS experience fly with No 3 Flying Training School at Cranwell for 75 hours over a period of 31 weeks. Trainees can expect to solo about six weeks into the Basic Flying Training course.

On completion of the Basic Flying Training course pilots are 'streamed' for the type of operational aircraft for which they are considered best suited: Group 1 (Fast Jet); Group 2 (Multi-engine); or Group 3 (Helicopters). Most newly-trained pilots are streamed for Fast Jets, since this is the RAF's primary operational requirement. For these an additional 61 hours training is given at the same FTS at which basic training was conducted.

These totals include a Flexibility Element to permit additional flying according to individual trainees' needs, and a further Incidental allowance provides for the completion of aborted flying sorties, test failures, or any lack of continuity in the training programme.

The Advanced Training phase is conducted according to the Group for which pilots have been streamed. Those destined for Fast Jets who will eventually fly Buccaneers, Harriers, Jaguars or Tornados in squadron service take an 85-hour Advanced Flying training course on British Aerospace Hawk T.Mk 1s at No 4 FTS, RAF Valley before leaving Support Command (under whose wings, if you will excuse a pun, all RAF pilot training is conducted), to be given 72 hours/16 weeks tactical and weapons training on Hawk T.Mk 1As at Nos 1 or 2 Tactical Weapons Units (TWU) at RAF Brawdy and RAF Chivenor. The TWUs give newly-qualified pilots experience of weapons usage before they move on to an Operational Conversion Unit (OCU) to train on the actual type of first-line aircraft to be flown on a squadron.

In time of crisis the TWUs and OCUs would play an active role, either as reinforcements for other squadrons operating the same type of aircraft or by assuming squadron status, to which end some have 'shadow squadron' status (see list below).

After basic training, Group 2 pilots undergo a further 27-hour, eight-week course on Jet Provost T.Mk 5As or Tucano T.Mk 1s before transferring to No 6 FTS at RAF Finningley for a 45-hour, eight-week course on British Aerospace Jetstream T.Mk 1 twin turboprop trainers. Group 3 pilots go straight to No 2 FTS at RAF Shawbury to complete 28 weeks' rotary wing training comprising 76 hours on Westland Gazelle HT Mk 3 and 50 hours on Westland Wessex HC Mk 2 helicopters. In each case conversion training at an appropriately-equipped OCU follows.

The complete RAF training pattern is illustrated by the following chart:

RAF Training and Operational Conversion Units

Unit	Aircraft type(s)	Station
Elementary Flying Training School Chipmunk T.Mk 10		RAF Swinderby
No 1 FTS	Tucano T.Mk 1*	RAF Linton-on-Ouse
No 2 FTS	Gazelle HT.Mk 3, Wessex HC Mk 2	RAF Shawbury
No 3 FTS	Tucano T.Mk 1*	RAF College Cranwell
No 4 FTS	Hawk T.Mk 1	RAF Valley
No 6 FTS	Dominie T.Mk 1, Jetstream T.Mk 1, Jet Provost T.Mk 5A	RAF Finningley
No 7 FTS	Tucano T.Mk 1*	RAF Church Fenton

* Replacing Jet Provost T.Mk 3A/5A during 1990/91.

226 OCU	Jaguar GR.Mk 1A/T.Mk 2A	RAF Lossiemouth
229 OCU	Tornado F.3	RAF Coningsby
231 OCU	Canberra B.Mk 2/T.Mk 4	RAF Wyton
233 OCU	Harrier GR.Mk 3/T.Mk 4	RAF Wittering
236 OCU	Nimrod MR.Mk 2	RAF St Mawgan

237 OCU	Buccaneer S.Mk 2A/B,	
	Hunter T.Mk 7/8	RAF Lossiemouth
240 OCU	Chinook HC.Mk 1, Puma HC.Mk 1	RAF Odiham
241 OCU	TriStar K.Mk 1, VC-10 C.Mk 1/K	
	Mk 2/3, BAe 146 CC.Mk 2	RAF Brize Norton
242 OCU	Hercules C.Mk 1/3	RAF Lyneham

Trinational Tornado Training Establishment	
Tornado GR.Mk1/1T	RAF Cottesmore
Tornado Weapons Conversion Unit	
Tornado GR. Mk 1	RAF Honington
SAR Training Squadron Wessex HC.Mk 2	RAF Valley

Central Flying School (Training of Qualified Flying Instructors) operates Bulldog T.Mk 1s, Jet Provost T.Mk 3A/5As, Tucano T.Mk 1s and Hawk T.Mk 1As from RAF Scampton, and Gazelle HT.Mk 3 helicopters from RAF Shawbury.

Direct entrant aircrew recruits assume the rank of Aircraftman (Officer Cadet) on entering the RAF, while graduates are commissioned as Pilot Officers.

There are two types of RAF Commission. A Permanent Commission, subject to satisfactory completion of all training phases, is to the age of 55, with an optional retirement date (ORD) at the earliest age of 38 or after completion of 16 years commissioned service, whichever comes later. It carries a pension which is index-linked from the age of 55. Short-Service Commissions, which are not overly emphasised by the RAF for pilot entrants because of the high cost of training and current pilot shortages, are for a period of 12 years, with an option to leave after eight years with a tax-free gratuity.

Promotion to Flying Officer and thence to Flight Lieutenant is automatic. A graduate entrant will typically reach the rank of Flight Lieutenant within two years of entry, and could be considered for promotion to the rank of Squadron Leader after his first tour of squadron duty, although such a promotion would not be likely to be granted immediately. A direct entrant takes about six years to achieve the rank of Flight Lieutenant. Promotion beyond that rank is subject to written examinations, with promotions decided on the merit of annual performance reports from squadron commanders.

Promotion to the rank of Squadron Leader and beyond can only be offered to holders of Permanent Commissions. There is also a Reserve Service requirement of four-years additional service in the event of recall during a national

Old and new. The RAF's long-serving Jet Provost T.5A basic trainers (background) are being replaced by Shorts Tucano T.1 turboprops such as this one from No.7 FTS at RAF Church Fenton. (Peter R. March)

After basic training, RAF pilots fly BAe Hawk T.1/1As for advanced and weapons training. (British Aerospace)

Where every would-be RAF pilot imagines himself one day: flying a Tornado F.3, the service's principal air defence fighter. (Author)

British Aerospace/McDonnell Douglas Harrier GR.5/7s are replacing the earlier Harrier GR.3 (background) with RAF V/STOL squadrons. This GR.5 one is from No.233 Operational Conversion Unit based at RAF Wittering, Cambridgeshire. (Ministry of Defence)

Boeing Vertol Chinook H.C.1 is the RAF's heavy lift helicopter.
(Boeing Helicopter Company)

Multi-engine training for RAF pilots is conducted on British Aerospace Jetstream twin turboprops from RAF Leeming in Yorkshire.

British Aerospace Nimrod MR.2 maritime reconnaissance aircraft. (Author)

Westland Gazelle helicopter lifting off for a training sortie at the Army Air Corps Centre, Middle Wallop. (Author)

emergency. The Permanent Commission carries a pension and a tax-free gratuity equal to three times the annual pension after 16 years of service. The RAF promotion ladder looks like this:

Pilot Officer
Flying Officer
Flight Lieutenant
Squadron Leader
Wing Commander
Group Captain
Air Commodore
Air Vice-Marshal
Air Marshal
Air Chief Marshal
Marshal of the RAF

Squadron Service

At the end of his Operational Conversion course the newly-trained RAF pilot gets his first appointment (known as a 'posting') to an operational RAF squadron, which is the Service's basic working unit. Pilots do get an opportunity to state a preference to a particular posting, but there is no guarantee that personal wishes can be accommodated. Tours of duty (that is, the period between postings) usually last about 30 months. To give some idea of the scope of the Royal Air Force in the 1990s and the geographical spread of operational squadrons within RAF Strike Command, the list below provides details of squadrons with the aircraft operated and their regular bases, although proposed defence cuts following the lessening of East-West tension and the aftermath of the Gulf War may substantially alter the pattern of RAF overseas deployments in the future. Strike Command is responsible for Strike/Attack and Offensive Support; Air Defence; Reconnaissance; Maritime Patrol and Anti-Submarine Attack; Search-and-Rescue; Transport; Aerial Refuelling and Helicopter operations.

Squadron	Aircraft type(s)	Station
(S) = Shadow Squadron		
No.1	Harrier GR5/GR7	RAF Wittering
No.2	Tornado GR1A	RAF Laarbruch (Germany)
No.3	Harrier GR5	RAF Gütersloh (Germany)

No.4	Harrier GR3/5	RAF Gütersloh (Germany)
No.5	Tornado F3	RAF Coningsby
No.6	Jaguar GR1A	RAF Coltishall
No.7	Chinook HC1	RAF Odiham
No.8	Shackleton AEW2 (Boeing Sentry AEW1 from 1991)	RAF Lossiemouth RAF Waddington
No.9	Tornado GR1	RAF Brüggen (Germany)
No.10	VC10 C1	RAF Brize Norton
No.11	Tornado F3	RAF Leeming
No.12	Buccaneer S2B	RAF Lossiemouth
No.13	Tornado GR1A	RAF Honington
No.14	Tornado GR1	RAF Brüggen (Germany)
No.15	Tornado GR1	RAF Laarbruch (Germany)
No.16	Tornado GR1	RAF Laarbruch (Germany)
No.17	Tornado GR1	RAF Brüggen (Germany)
No.18	Chinook HC1	RAF Gütersloh (Germany)
No.19	Phantom FGR2	RAF Wildenrath (Germany)
No.20	Tornado GR1	RAF Laarbruch (Germany)
No.22	Wessex HC2	RAF Finningley and detachments
No.23	Tornado F3	RAF Leeming
No.24	Hercules C1/C3	RAF Lyneham
No.25	Tornado F3	RAF Leeming
No.27	Tornado GR1	RAF Marham
No.28	Wessex HC2	RAF Sek Kong, Hong Kong
No.29	Tornado F3	RAF Coningsby
No.30	Hercules C1/C3	RAF Lyneham
No.31	Tornado GR1	RAF Brüggen (Germany)
No.32	Andover CC2, BAe 125 C1/C2/C3, Gazelle HT3/HC4	RAF Northolt
No.33	Puma HC1	RAF Odiham
No.38	Nimrod MR2	RAF St Mawgan
No.41	Jaguar GR1A	RAF Coltishall

No.42	Nimrod MR2	RAF St Mawgan
No.43	Tornado F3	RAF Leuchars
No.45(S)	Tornado GR1	RAF Honington
No.47	Hercules C1/C3	RAF Lyneham
No.51	Nimrod R1	RAF Wyton
No.54	Jaguar GR1A	RAF Coltishall
No.55	Victor K2	RAF Marham
No.56	Phantom FGR2	RAF Wattisham
No.60	Andover C1/CC2	RAF Wildenrath (Germany)
No.63(S)	Hawk T1A	RAF Chivenor
No.64(S)	Phantom FGR2	RAF Leuchars
No.65(S)	Tornado F3	RAF Coningsby
No.70	Hercules C1/C3	RAF Lyneham
No.72	Wessex HC2	Aldergrove Airport, Northern Ireland
No.74	Phantom FG1	RAF Wattisham
No.78	Chinook HC1, Sea King HAR3	Mount Pleasant, Falkland Islands
No.79(S)	Hawk T1A	RAF Brawdy
No.84	Wessex HU5C	RAF Akrotiri (Cyprus)
No.92	Phantom FGR2	RAF Wildenrath (Germany)
No.100	Canberra (various marks)	RAF Wyton
No.101	VC-10 K2/3	RAF Brize Norton
No.111	Tornado F3	RAF Leuchars
No.115	Andover E3	RAF Benson
No.120	Nimrod MR2	RAF Kinloss
No.151(S)	Hawk T1A	RAF Chivenor
No.201	Nimrod MR2	RAF Kinloss
No.202	Sea King HAR3	RAF Finningley and detachments
No.206	Nimrod MR2	RAF Kinloss
No.208	Buccaneer S2	RAF Lossiemouth
No.216	TriStar K1/KC1	RAF Brize Norton
No.230	Puma HC1	RAF Gütersloh (Germany)
No.234(S)	Hawk T1A	RAF Brawdy
No.360	Canberra T17	RAF Wyton
No.617	Tornado GR1	RAF Marham

The Air Training Corps

The Air Training Corps, motto *Venture Adventure,* was formed in 1941 to provide pre-entry training for boys planning careers with the Royal Air Force or Fleet Air Arm. After the war the Corps was remodelled and its scope expanded, so that its present day function as a voluntary youth organisation open to boys and girls is to encourage a practical interest in aviation, adventure and sport which will be useful in either service or civilian life.

Age limits for joining the ATC are 13 to 18 years, though cadets can remain in the Corps until they reach the age of 20, after which many become staff or instructors within the Corps. The establishment of the ATC is for a maximum of 40,000 cadets supervised by up to 9,000 adult staff, administered from Headquarters Air Cadets at RAF Newton, Nottinghamshire. There are seven ATC regions:

Region	Headquarters
Scotland	RAF Turnhouse
North & East	RAF Linton-on-Ouse
Central & East	RAF Henlow
London & South East	RAF Northolt
South West	RAF Locking
Wales	RAF St. Athan
North & West	RAF Sealand

These regions administer 40 Wings, and approximately 1,000 Squadrons and Detached Flights.

A principal function of the Air Training Corps is to provide flying experience for ATC cadets and for cadets from the Combined Cadet Force (RAF), via the RAF's Air Experience Flights (AEFs — see below), and Volunteer Gliding Schools, of which there are 28, making the Air Cadet Gliding Organisation the largest glider training organisation in the world.

The Air Experience Flights are located at RAF Manston, Bournemouth International Airport, Bristol-Filton Aerodrome, Exeter Airport, Cambridge Airport, RAF Abingdon, RAF Newton, RAF Shawbury, RAF Finningley, RAF Woodvale, RAF Leeming, RAF Turnhouse and RAF Sydenham. Their fleet of powered aircraft is made up of de Havilland Chipmunk trainers, and a British Aerospace Bulldog. The AEFs' aim is to give each eligible ATC or CCF(RAF) cadet one 25-minute flight per year.

The Air Cadet Gliding Organisation has a fleet of 40

Slingsby Venture Mk 2 motor gliders which are being replaced from the spring of 1990 by 53 all-composite Grob G.109B Vigilant Mk 1s; 100 Grob 103 Viking gliders for training and solo flying; plus four ASW-19 Valiant and two Janus C high performance sailplanes for advanced soaring and competition flying. The fleet is dispersed at the Air Corps Central Gliding School at RAF Syerston and at the Volunteer Gliding Schools listed below. Each year some 1,800 ATC and CCF cadets complete glider training to solo standard and gain their wings (after 16th birthday) on the Air Cadets Gliding Organisation fleet.

ATC Gliding Organisation Schools

No of School	Location
Central Gliding School	RAF Syerston, Nottinghamshire
611 VGS	Swanton Morley, Norfolk
612 VGS	Benson, Oxfordshire
613 VGS	Halton, Buckinghamshire
614 VGS	Wethersfield, Essex
615 VGS	Kenley, Surrey
616 VGS	Henlow, Bedfordshire
617 VGS	Manston, Kent
618 VGS	West Malling, Kent
621 VGS	Weston-super-Mare, Avon
622 VGS	Upavon, Wiltshire
624 VGS	Chivenor, Devon
625 VGS	South Cerney, Gloucestershire
626 VGS	Predannack, Cornwall
631 VGS	Sealand, Cheshire
632 VGS	Ternhill, Shropshire
633 VGS	Cosford, Shropshire
634 VGS	St. Athan, South Glamorgan
635 VGS	Samlesbury, Lancashire
636 VGS	Swansea, West Glamorgan
637 VGS	Little Rissington, Gloucestershire
642 VGS	Linton-on-Ouse, Yorkshire
643 VGS	Scampton, Lincolnshire
644 VGS	Syerston, Nottinghamshire
645 VGS	Catterick, Yorkshire
661 VGS	Kirknewton, Lothian

662 VGS	Arbroath, Tayside
663 VGS	Kinloss, Morayshire
664 VGS	Bishop's Court, Northern Ireland

In addition to the Air Experience Flights and Volunteer Gliding schools the Air Training Corps operates several other schemes for getting cadets into the air. An Opportunity Flights scheme run in conjunction with commercial airlines enables cadets to 'sit in' on scheduled services when space permits. Several hundred cadets make such flights each year. The ATC Overseas Flights scheme provides an opportunity for cadets to travel on RAF Support Command transport flights on Hercules, TriStar and VC-10 aircraft, usually on routes to Cyprus, Germany and Gibraltar. Other opportunity flights are arranged on an ad hoc basis in service aircraft, airliners and company-owned and private aeroplanes.

Perhaps the most important of the flying schemes administered by the Air Training Corps is the Ministry of Defence (formerly Royal Air Force and Royal Navy) Flying Scholarship which provides 30 hours' free flying instruction at selected civilian flying schools. Some 25-30 flying schools and clubs participate in the scheme, which is the largest sponsored flying programme in the United Kingdom. To apply for a Scholarship one need not necessarily be a member of the ATC or CCF, and since the autumn of 1989 girl applicants have been accepted as a result of the RAF's new policy to recruit female pilots and navigators. The broad requirements are that applicants should have reached the age of 17 years by the start of their training courses, which are conducted in the Easter (March/April) and Summer (June/September) school holidays; hold GCSE or equivalent passes at Ordinary Level in English language, Mathematics and three other subjects, only one of which may be non-academic; and be able to take up the offer of training within 12 months.

Short-listed candidates undergo a two-and-a-half day pre-assessment screening at the Officer and Aircrew Selection Centre, presently at RAF Biggin Hill, but due to be moved to RAF Cranwell, where medical fitness and personal and pilot aptitudes are examined to the same standard required for entry into the RAF as aircrew. Those who pass the OASC selection procedure enter the Final Selection competition.

The 30-hour Scholarship course takes about 28 days to complete and includes about 8–10 hours of solo flying in modern light training aircraft. The cost of the flying instruction, board and lodging is paid by the Ministry of Defence. Those who successfully complete the course and pass flying tests and ground examinations receive a certificate (cadets also receive a Flying Scholarship 'wings' badge), and may continue with their training at their own expense to complete the necessary minimum 40 hours for the issue of a civilian Private Pilot Licence (see Chapter Two).

The number of MoD Scholarships awarded each year averages 540. About two-thirds of Scholarship winners go on to obtain their PPLs.

The MoD Flying Scholarship scheme does not impose any obligation on successful candidates to join the RAF (though about one-third of Scholarship winners do go on to RAF air-crew careers) nor does it offer any guarantee of subsequent acceptance for service flying training.

Another flying opportunity for Air Cadets is the Pilot Navigation Training Scheme, which provides a two-week course including ten hours' flying training on Chipmunk aircraft with an Air Experience Flight.

The Royal Navy

Like the Royal Air Force, the Royal Navy also has a two-tier system for recruiting aircrew officers, either through the Dartmouth Naval College in Devon or by Direct Graduate entry. Nationality requirements are the same as those for the RAF detailed above, but the Navy's entry-age limits for trainee pilots are 17-26 years of age, and candidates must also be between 162-198 centimetres in height (and have "teeth adequate for the efficient mastication of food", it says on the application form!). Initial aptitude testing for would-be Navy pilots is again conducted at the Officer and Aircrew Selection Centre at RAF Biggin Hill, followed by a two-day selection session with the Admiralty Interview Board at HMS Sultan (a shore base, not a ship) at Gosport in Hampshire. Those candidates recommended for a Commission undergo a medical examination by the Central Air Medical Board at nearby Fareham. The final selection of short-listed applicants is made by the Ministry of Defence's Final Selection Committee. The Committee convenes some six to eight weeks before each point of entry to the Britannia Naval College at Dartmouth.

Those recruits who enter the Service via the Naval College assume the rank of Midshipman. Graduates take the rank of Acting Sub-Lieutenant. Both categories of entrant follow the same initial training pattern with two terms at Dartmouth undergoing practical training at sea and gaining air experience on de Havilland Chipmunk trainers at Plymouth Airport before commencing their Elementary Flying Course, which is conducted in RAF Bulldog trainers of the Royal Navy Elementary Flying Training School at RAF Topcliffe. The EFT course lasts 20 weeks and provides 75 hours of training.

Because the number of fixed-wing, carrier-based aircraft in the Royal Navy's inventory has been much reduced, most Fleet Air Arm pilots now fly helicopters, and there are very limited opportunities for fixed-wing pilots for the BAe Sea Harrier STOVL jets which serve aboard the Royal Navy's three aircraft carriers, HMS *Illustrious, Invincible* and *Ark Royal*.

Royal Navy pilots streamed for Harrier flying move from RAF Topcliffe to Cranwell for training on RAF Jet Provosts or Tucanos before proceeding to RAF Valley and RAF Brawdy for advanced training and weapons training on BAe Hawks, and finally to RNAS Yeovilton for conversion and operational training on the Sea Harrier.

Helicopter pilots move from RAF Topcliffe to RNAS Culdrose in Cornwall for a further 18-week, 80-hour training course on Westland Gazelle helicopters. Operational training for helicopter fliers is carried out at Portland on Lynx and Sea King helicopters, or at Yeovilton on the Lynx, preparing for specific roles such as anti-submarine warfare.

A Flying Badge is awarded to those who successfully complete their initial training phases at Culdrose or RAF Cranwell, usually about ten months after the start of flying training. New pilot entrants can expect to reach operational status with the Royal Navy some two and a half years after joining the service. Aircrew are not normally permitted to leave the service until at least five years after the award of their Flying Badge.

The Royal Navy offers two types of Commission for aircrew officers. A pensionable Medium Career Commission lasts 16 years or to the age of 38 years, whichever is the later. A Short Career Commission lasts 12 years with an option to leave the service after eight years with a tax-free gratuity but no pension.

Promotion within the Royal Navy is not tied to any particular stage in pilot training. A Midshipman entrant is promoted to Sub-Lieutenant (Acting or Confirmed status according to whether flying training has been completed or not) after two years' service. He should reach the rank of Lieutenant some five years after entry, although this can be reduced if seniority gains have been won during training. Graduates, who assume the rank of Acting Sub-Lieutenant, are confirmed in that rank on completion of operational flying training, unless they have already won promotion to Lieutenant in the meanwhile. There are opportunities for officers holding Short or Medium Career Commissions to convert these to Full Career Commissions within the four-to-nine years service period, although those who show outstanding ability may be given the opportunity to take a Full Career Commission earlier. Full Career transfer officers are automatically promoted to Lieutenant-Commander on achieving eight years' seniority. Promotion beyond the rank of Lieutenant-Commander is competitive, on merit.

The British Army

The British Army is unique among the peacetime services in offering pilot careers to non-commissioned officers. However, it does not, like the Royal Air Force and Royal Navy, recruit pilots directly into the Army Air Corps from civilian life, but takes volunteers from other arms of the Service. No new recruit can therefore join the Army for the express purpose (or with the certainty) of getting pilot training. Even potential recruits with civilian PPL (Helicopter) licences are of no special interest to the Army, which expects its pilots to be soldiers first and foremost, and aviators second.

The Army's policy of NCO aircrew recruitment does give those lacking the RAF or RN's aircrew educational standards a chance to become pilots. Do not think, however, that 'other ranks' are second-class pilots. Far from it. NCO pilots with the Army Air Corps must display quite exceptional aptitude. They are invariably highly motivated and they are very highly thought of in the Service. Since NCO pilots do not have the administrative responsibilities of officers they also tend to build flying hours and gain experience more quickly.

NCO pilots come from two sources: either as direct entrant soldiers to the Army Air Corps, or by voluntary transfer. All recruits get their basic Army training at Catterick Camp, North Yorkshire, after which they move on to Leconfield or to Aldershot to take a course in Heavy Goods Vehicle Driving. There follows a ground crewman training course at Army Air Corps Headquarters at Middle Wallop in Hampshire. When opportunities for pilot training arise, five times each year with courses of 16 people, divided roughly equally between NCOs and Officers, potential pilot trainees are screened at the Officer and Aircrew Selection Centre. Those who pass the tests but do not score outstandingly may be selected for training as aircrewmen/observers with the possibility of future selection for pilot training. The aircrewman/observer course includes some 16 hours pure flying instruction on Gazelle light helicopters, providing the crewman with enough knowledge to land the machine successfully should his pilot be injured or otherwise incapacitated, the remainder of the course being devoted to technical servicing and maintenance, gunnery and forward air control techniques, observation and reconnaissance, and especially, navigation and map reading at high speed and low level, typically in excess of 100 knots at 50 feet, which is the lowest level at which military helicopters can safely operate in the European Theatre without dangerous exposure to groundfire. The aircrewman is thus well versed in all aspects of helicopter operation at the end of his training, which continues through his first regimental posting, where he gains practical experience of air gunnery and anti-tank operations — vital roles of the Army's helicopters.

There are four basic means of entry for Army officers: Regular Commissions and 'Young Entry' Special Regular Commissions (Reg C and SRC); Special Regular Commissions (SRC); Short-Service Commissions (SSC); and Graduate entry. Candidates for Regular Commissions may apply for pilot training before entering the Royal Military Academy at Sandhurst. They must be aged between 17¾ and

22 years on joining and have a minimum of five GCSE Orindary Level passes — including two Advanced Level passes — which must include English language, mathematics and a science subject or a foreign language. For 'Young Entry' Special Regular Commissions (age under 22 years on entry) the Advanced Level GCSEs are not essential. Pilot training for those selected commences after completion of Standard Military and Regular Career courses at the RMA, Sandhurst, but the commission is not confirmed until the flying course has been completed. Those who fail to finish the course are transferred to another branch of the Service.

The age limits for Special Regular Commissions (Middle Entry) are 20-26 years with five Ordinary Level passes in GCSE, and for Short-Service Commissions 17½-26 years. Short-Service entrants take only the Standard Military Course at Sandhurst before beginning flying training. University graduates may apply for any of these commissions (subject to the age limits). All commissions are probationary until flying training has been satisfactorily completed. Short-Service Commissions are for a minimum service period of five years, which can be extended to eight years. Some 90 percent of the officer aircrew joining the Army Air Corps transfer from within the service, having completed training and three years service in other arms before starting flying. All officers completing the SMC and RCC courses at RMA Sandhurst spend six months on attachment to an Infantry Battalion before going to AAC Headquarters at Middle Wallop to begin flying training.

The Army Air Corps' pilot training course consists of a 40-hour Elementary Flying course on fixed-wing de Havilland Chipmunk aircraft, which brings trainees up to Private Pilot Licence standard. NCO pilot trainees take a five-week Pre-Pilot's Course to adapt them to the rigours of groundschool before starting flight training proper. The Basic Rotary course comprises 80 hours flying over a three-month period. The Advanced Course consists of 80-100 hours flying on Gazelles during which the special role of Army helicopter operations is emphasized. Learning to direct artillery fire from the air for forward air control duties, and observation/reconnaissance are major aspects of this phase of training, at the end of which AAC pilots receive their Wings. Other than his aircrewmen, the newly qualified pilot may not carry any passengers until he has completed a further 50 hours flying and been checked out by an Army Qualified Helicopter Flying Instructor. He is accepted as a fully qualified helicopter pilot typically with about 235 helicopter hours in his logbook. In operational service an Officer Pilot with the Army Air Corps can expect to log 1,000-1,200 flying hours in a three-year tour of duty. Free of the administrative duties of officers, the NCO pilot will log perhaps 50 per cent more.

In Civvy Street . . .
What of the prospects for military pilots when they leave the services? In general they are very good, with heavy demand for former service fliers by airlines and flying training establishments. Foreign governments, particular those in the Middle East with friendly relations with Britain and British aircraft manufacturers, also place high value on former UK military personnel, and accordingly offer attractive short-term employment packages to those suitably qualified.

Bear in mind that all three British armed forces demand minimum commitments of anything from six years upwards, which is entirely reasonably considering the immense cost of training. On leaving the services resettlement grants are payable which many ex-military pilots use to gain civilian flying licences — essential to obtain employment in the commercial field no matter what military qualifications may be held. Professional flying schools (see Chapters 3 and 4) run specially-developed courses for ex-service aircrew, who are usually permitted to count flight time logged in the forces towards an exemption from the full Commercial Pilot's Licence course. The Civil Aviation Authority will advise on specific requirements necessary in each individual case to gain the civilian licences or ratings.

Bear in mind though, that as a reason for seeking a service career the prospect of subsequently getting a civilian flying job later is unlikely to endear candidates to selection boards!

Private Pilot Training Schools & Clubs (fixed-wing aircraft)

LONDON AREA

Air Touring Club, The Blue Hangar, Biggin Hill Airport, Near Westerham, Kent. Tel: 0959 73133

Alouette Flying Club, Building 332, Biggin Hill Airport, Near Westerham, Kent. Tel: 0959 73243

BHSF Cessna Flight Centre, Biggin Hill, Westerham, Kent. Tel: 0959 73419

Biggin Hill School of Flying, Biggin Hill Airport, Near Westerham, Kent TN16 3BN. Tel: 0959 73583

Blackbushe School of Flying, Blackbushe Airport, Camberley, Surrey GU17 9LQ. Tel: 0252 870999

British Airways Flying Club, Wycombe Air Park, Booker, Near Marlow, Buckinghamshire SL7 3DR. Tel: 0494 29262

Cabair Flying Training, Biggin Hill Airport, Westerham, Kent. Tel: 0959 73583.

Civil Air Flying Club, Building 160, Biggin Hill Airport, Near Westerham, Kent TN16 3BN. Tel: 0959 73853

Denham Cessna Flight Centre, Denham Aerodrome, Denham, Buckinghamshire. Tel: 0895 834730

Denham School of Flying, Denham Aerodrome, Denham, Buckinghamshire UB9 5DE. Tel: 0895 833327

Fairoaks Flight Centre, Fairoaks Aerodrome, Near Chobham, Surrey GU24 8HU. Tel: 027685 8075

Firecrest Aviation, Leavesden Airport, Near Watford, Hertfordshire. Tel: 0923 662794

Kingair Flying Club, Biggin Hill Airport, Near Westerham, Kent. Tel: 0959 75088

Leavesden Flight Centre, Leavesden Aerodrome, Near Watford, Hertfordshire WD2 7BY. Tel: 0923 671411

London Flight Centre, Headcorn Aerodrome, Lashenden, Kent. Tel: 0622 890997

London School of Flying, Elstree Aerodrome, Borehamwood, Hertfordshire WD6 3AW. Tel: 081 953 4343

Panshanger School of Flying, Panshanger Aerodrome, Near Welwyn Garden City, Hertfordshire SG14 2NH. Tel: 0707 335021

Redhill Flying Club, Redhill Aerodrome, Surrey RH1 5JY. Tel: 0737 822959

Stapleford Flying Club, Stapleford Aerodrome, Near Romford, Essex RM4 1SJ. Tel: 04028 380

Surrey & Kent Flying Club, Biggin Hill Airport, Kent TN16 3BN.
Tel: 0959 72255

Three Counties Flying Club, Blackbushe Airport, Near Camberley,
Surrey. Tel: 0252 873747

Wycombe Air Centre, Wycombe Air Park, Booker, Near Marlow,
Buckinghamshire SL7 3DR. Tel: 0494 443737

SOUTH
Abbas Air, Compton Abbas Airfield, Compton Abbas, Near
Shaftesbury, Dorset. Tel: 0747 811767

Airbourne Flying School, Sandown Airport, Isle of Wight.
Tel: 0983 403355

Air South, Shed Eleven, Shoreham Airport, Sussex BN4 5FF.
Tel: 0273 462874

Bournemouth Flying Club, Building 198, Bournemouth-Hurn Airport,
Christchurch, Dorset BH23 6HA. Tel: 0202 578558

Carill Aviation Flying School, Southampton Airport, Eastleigh,
Hampshire. Tel: 0703 643528

Compton Abbas Airfield, Compton Abbas, Near Shaftesbury, Dorset.
Tel: 0747 811767

Goodwood Flying School, Goodwood Airfield, Near Chichester,
West Sussex PO18 0PH. Tel: 0243 774656

Interair Flight Centre, Hangar 62, North Side, Bournemouth-Hurn
Airport, Christchurch, Dorset. Tel: 0202 581001

Mercury Flying Club, Hangar One, Shoreham Airport,
Shoreham-by-Sea, Sussex BN4 5FF. Tel: 0273 462277

SFT Aviation, Bournemouth-Hurn Airport, Christchurch, Dorset
BH23 6DB. Tel: 0202 499888

Southern Aero Club, Shoreham Airport, Shoreham-by-Sea, Sussex.
Tel: 0273 462457

Southern Air, Shoreham Airport, Shoreham-by-Sea, Sussex.
Tel: 0273 461661

Thruxton Flight Centre, Thruxton Aerodrome, Weyhill, Near Andover,
Hampshire SP11 8PW. Tel: 0264 772508

Vectair Aviation, Goodwood Airfield, Near Chichester, West Sussex.
Tel: 0243 781652

Wiltshire Aeroplane Club, Old Sarum Airfield, Near Salisbury, Wiltshire.
Tel: 0722 23385

SOUTH WEST
Airways Flight Training, Building 12, Exeter Airport, Devon.
Tel: 0392 64216

Bristol Flying Centre, Bristol-Lulsgate Airport, Bristol, Avon BS19 3DP.
Tel: 027 587 4501

Bristol & Wessex Aeroplane Club, Bristol-Lulsgate Airport, Bristol, Avon BS19 3EP. Tel: 027 587 2514

Cornwall Flying Club, Bodmin Airfield, Cardinham, Bodmin, Cornwall PL30 4BU. Tel: 020 882 419

Devon School of Flying, Dunkeswell Aerodrome, Near Honiton, Devon EX14 0RA. Tel: 0404 891643

Exeter Flying Centre, Exeter Airport, Clyst Honiton, Devon EX5 2BA. Tel: 0392 67653

Land's End Aero Club, Land's End Aerodrome, St. Just, Penzance, Cornwall. Tel: 0736 788771

SOUTH EAST
Andrewsfield Flying Club, Saling Airfield, Stebbing, Great Dunmow, Essex CM6 3TH. Tel: 0371 86744

Clacton Aero Club, Clacton Airfield, West Road, Clacton, Essex. Tel: 0255 424671

Essex Flying School, The Hangar, Earls Colne Aerodrome, Colchester, Essex. Tel: 0787 223676

Leading-Edge Aviation, Southend Airport, Southend-on-Sea, Essex. Tel: 0702 544057

London Flight Centre, Lydd Airport, Romney Marsh, Kent. Tel: 0679 21549

London Flight Centre, Stansted Airport, Bishop's Stortford, Essex. Tel: 0279 815579

Rochester Aviation, Rochester Airport, Medway, Kent. Tel: 0634 816340

Seawing Flying Club, Eastern Perimeter Road, Southend Airport, Southend-on-Sea, Essex SS2 6YF. Tel: 0702 545420

Skylane Flight Centre, Southend Airport, Southend-on-Sea, Essex SS2 6YF. Tel: 0702 546156

South East College of Air Training, Lydd Airport, Romney Marsh, Kent. Tel: 0679 21236

Southend Flying Club, Southend Airport, Southend-on-Sea, Essex SS2 6YF. Tel: 0702 545198

Thames Estuary Flying Club, Southend Airport, Southend-on-Sea, Essex. Tel: 0702 545415

Thanet Flying Club, Manston Airport, Near Ramsgate, Kent. Tel: 0843 823520

EAST ANGLIA
Arrow Air Centre, Shipham Airfield, Thetford, Norfolk IP25 7SB. Tel: 0362 820162

Cambridge Aero Club, Cambridge Airport, Teversham, Cambridge CB5 8RX. Tel: 0223 61133 Ext. 3214

Cambridge Flying Group, Cambridge Airport, Teversham, Cambridge CB5 8RX. Tel: 02205 3343

Fenland Aero Club, Fenland Airfield, Holbeach St. John's, Lincolnshire. Tel: 0406 34461

Horizon Flying Club, Ipswich Airport, Nacton Road, Ipswich, Suffolk IP3 9QF. Tel: 0473 714840

Ipswich School of Flying, Ipswich Airport, Ipswich, Suffolk IP3 9QF. Tel: 0473 729510

Norfolk & Norwich Aero Club, The Club House, RAF Swanton Morley, Near Dereham, Norfolk NR20 4LW. Tel: 036 283 274

Norwich School of Flying, Norwich Airport, Norfolk. Tel: 0603 403107

Rural Flying Corps, Bourn Aerodrome, Cambridge CB3 7TQ. Tel: 0954 719602

Suffolk Aero Club, Ipswich Airport, Nacton Road, Ipswich, Suffolk IP3 9QF. Tel: 0473 713312

MIDLANDS, CENTRAL, EAST & WEST
Aeros Flying Club, Staverton Airport, Cheltenham, Gloucestershire GL51 6SR. Tel: 0452 857419

Bobbington Air Training School, Halfpenny Green Aerodrome, Near Stourbridge, West Midlands. Tel: 038 488 292

Cotswold Aero Club, Staverton Airport, Cheltenham, Gloucestershire. Tel: 0452 713924

Coventry Aeroplane Club, Coventry Airport, Baginton, Warwickshire CV8 3AZ. Tel: 0203 301428

Donair Flying Club, East Midlands Airport, Castle Donington, Derbyshire DE7 2SA. Tel: 0332 810444

East Midlands Flying School, East Midlands Airport, Castle Donington, Derbyshire DE7 2SA. Tel: 0332 850383

Enstone Flying Club, Enstone Aerodrome, Enstone, Oxfordshire. Tel: 0608 677208

Gloucestershire Flying Centre, Staverton Airport, Cheltenham, Gloucestershire GL51 6SR. Tel: 0452 713555

Gloucester & Cheltenham School of Flying, Staverton Airport, Cheltenham, Gloucestershire. Tel: 0452 857153

G&B Aviation, Coventry Airport, Baginton, Coventry, Warwickshire. Tel: 0203 305721

Herefordshire Aero Club, Shobdon Airfield, Leominster, Herefordshire HR6 9NR. Tel: 056 881 369

Humber Flying Club, Hillsboro House, Town Road, Tetney, Grimsby DN36 5JD. Tel: 0652 680746

Klingair Flying Club, Peterborough Business Airport (Conington), Holme, Peterborough, Cambridgeshire PE7 3PX. Tel: 0487 832022

Leicestershire Aero Club, Leicester Airport, Gartree Road, Leicester LE2 2FG. Tel: 053 759 2360

Lincoln Aero Club, Sturgate Aerodrome, Near Gainsborough, Lincolnshire. Tel: 0522 721411

Luton Flight Training, Luton Airport, Luton, Bedfordshire. Tel: 0582 24426

Mercia Flight Training, Coventry Airport, Coventry CV8 3AZ. Tel: 0203 307003

Midland Air Training School, Coventry Airport, Baginton, Warwickshire CV8 3AZ. Tel: 0203 304914

Northamptonshire School of Flying, Sywell Aerodrome, Northamptonshire NN6 0BU. Tel: 0604 644678

Osprey Flying Club, Cranfield Airport, Cranfield, Bedfordshire. Tel: 0234 750197

Oxford Air Training School PPL Flight, Oxford Airport, Kidlington, Oxfordshire OX5 1RA. Tel: 0865 841234 Ext. 260

Phoenix Aviation, Cranfield Airport, Cranfield, Bedfordshire. Tel: 0234 750592

Sandwell Valley Aero Club, Coventry Airport, Baginton, Warwickshire. Tel: 0922 648556

Senair, Coventry Airport, Baginton, Warwickshire. Tel: 0203 302553

Sherwood Flying Club, Tollerton Airport, Nottinghamshire NG12 1BD. Tel: 0602 332334

Shropshire Aero Club, Sleap Airfield, Myddle, Shropshire. Tel: 0939 32882

Skegness Air Taxis Ltd, Skegness Aerodrome, Ingoldmells, Lincolnshire PE25 1JN. Tel: 0754 2240

Solihull Flying Club, Coventry Airport, Baginton, Warwickshire. Tel: 0564 826235

Solo Flight Captain's Club, Humberside Airport, Kirmington, South Humberside. Tel: 0652 688833

South Warwickshire Flying School, Wellesbourne Mountford Aerodrome, Warwickshire CV35 9EU. Tel: 0789 840094

Staverton Flying School, Staverton Airport, Near Cheltenham, Gloucestershire GL51 6SR. Tel: 0452 712388

Stratford Air Services, Wellesbourne Mountford Aerodrome, Near Stratford on Avon, Warwickshire CV35 9EU. Tel: 0789 842078

Trumanair, Flying School, Tollerton Airport, Nottinghamshire NG12 4GA. Tel: 0602 811327

Walkbury Flying Club, Sibson Aerodrome, Near Peterborough, Cambridgeshire. Tel: 0832 280289

Warwickshire Flying Training Centre, Birmingham Airport,
West Midlands B26 3QN. Tel: 021 782 7755

Wellesbourne Aviation, Wellesbourne Mountford Aerodrome,
Near Stratford on Avon, Warwickshire CV35 9EU. Tel: 0789 841066

Wickenby Flying Club, Wickenby Airfield, Langworth, Lincolnshire.
Tel: 06735 345

NORTH
ANT Flying Club, Blackpool Airport, Squires Gate, Lancashire
FY4 2QS. Tel: 0253 45396

Blackpool Air Centre, Blackpool Airport, Squires Gate, Lancashire.
Tel: 0253 41871

Carlisle Flight Centre, Carlisle Airport, Cumbria CA6 4NW.
Tel: 0228 73333

Cheshire Air Training School, Liverpool Airport, Hangar 3, Speke,
Liverpool, Lancashire L24 8QQ. Tel: 051 486 8383

Cleveland Flying School, Teesside Airport, Darlington, County Durham.
Tel: 0325 332855

Comed Aviation, Building 28, Blackpool Airport, Squires Gate,
Lancashire FY4 2QY. Tel: 02532 49072

Doncaster Aero Club, Doncaster Airport, Bawtry Road, Doncaster,
Yorkshire DN5 4HU. Tel: 0302 535666

Hull Aero Club, Brough Aerodrome, North Humberside.
Tel: 0482 667985

Lancashire Aero Club, Barton Aerodrome, Eccles, Lancashire M30 7SA.
Tel: 061 789 4785

Liverpool Flying School, No 4 Hangar, Liverpool Airport, Speke,
Liverpool L24 8QQ. Tel: 051 427 7449

MSF Aviation, Manchester International Airport, Wilmslow, Cheshire.
Tel: 061 499 1444

Newcastle upon Tyne Aero Club, Newcastle Airport, Woolsington,
Newcastle NE13 8BT. Tel: 091 286 1321

Ravenair, Hangar S22 Southside, Manchester International Airport,
Wilmslow, Cheshire SK9 4LL. Tel: 061 489 3139

Sandtoft Air Services, Sandtoft Aerodrome, Belton, Doncaster, South
Yorkshire DN9 1PN. Tel: 0427 873676

Sheffield Aero Club, Netherthorpe Aerodrome, Thorpe Salvin, Worksop
S80 3JQ. Tel: 0909 475233

Sherburn Aero Club, Sherburn-in-Elmet Aerodrome, Leeds, Yorkshire
LS25 6JE. Tel: 0977 682674

Teesside Aero Club, Teesside Airport, County Durham DL2 1NJ.
Tel: 0325 332752

Walker Air Training Services, Liverpool Airport, Speke, Liverpool, Lancashire. Tel: 051 448 1317

Westair Flying School, Blackpool Airport, Squires Gate, Blackpool FY4 2QX. Tel: 0253 404925

West Lancashire Aero Club, RAF Woodvale, Formby, Merseyside. Tel: 07048 72610

Woodvale Aviation, RAF Woodvale, Formby, Merseyside. Tel: 07048 74456

Yorkshire Aeroplane Club, Leeds-Bradford Airport, Yeadon, Leeds, Yorkshire LS19 7TU. Tel: 0532 503840

WALES
Cambrian Flying Club, Swansea Airport, West Glamorgan. Tel: 0792 297275

Cardiff Flying Centre Ltd, Cardiff-Wales Airport. Tel: 0446 711942

Cardiff-Wales Flying Club, Cardiff-Rhoose Airport. Tel: 0446 710000

Falcon Aero Club, Swansea Airport, West Glamorgan. Tel: 0792 205241

Flight-Aids Aero Club, Swansea Airport, West Glamorgan. Tel: 0792 297833

Haverfordwest School of Flying, Haverfordwest Aerodrome, Dyfed. Tel: 0437 760822

Mona Flying Club, RAF Mona, Anglesey, Tel: 0407 720581

SCOTLAND
Aberdeen Flying Club, Wellheads Drive, Aberdeen-Dyce Airport, Aberdeen AB2 0GQ. Tel: 0224 725333

Cumbernauld Flight Centre, Cumbernauld Airfield, Napier Road, Wardpark North, Cumbernauld G68 0EF. Tel: 0236 722100

Edinburgh Air Centre, Edinburgh Airport. Tel: 031 339 4059

Edinburgh Flying Club, Turnhouse Road, Edinburgh Airport EH12 0AL. Tel: 031 339 4990

Fife Aero Club, Fife Airport, Glenrothes, Fife KY6 2SL. Tel: 0592 753792

Glasgow Flying Club, Glasgow Airport, Abbotsinch Road, Paisley PA3 2RY. Tel: 041 889 4565

Highland Aero Club, Inverness (Dalcross) Airport, Inverness IV1 2JD. Tel: 0667 62230

Prestwick Flight Centre, Prestwick Airport, Ayr KA9 2SA. Tel: 0292 76523

Renfrew Flying Club, Glasgow Airport, Paisley. Tel: 041 887 3398

Scottish Airways Flyers, Prestwick Airport, Ayr. Tel: 0292 75583

Tayside Flying Club, Dundee (Riverside) Airport. Tel: 0382 644372

Turnhouse Flying Club, Edinburgh Airport, Edinburgh EH12 0AN.
Tel: 031 339 4706

West of Scotland Flying Club, Glasgow Airport, Paisley.
Tel: 041 889 7151

ISLE OF MAN
Ashley Gardener School of Flying, Ronaldsway Airport. Tel: 0624 823454

Manx Flyers Aero Club, 27 Club House, Derbyhaven, Castletown.
Tel: 0624 822926

CHANNEL ISLANDS
Channel Aviation, Guernsey Airport, St. Peter, Guernsey.
Tel: 0481 37217

Guernsey Flying Training, Guernsey Airport. Tel: 0481 65267

Jersey Aero Club, States Airport, Jersey. Tel: 0534 43990

Stratair Flight Training, Devereux House, Val Fontaine, Alderney.
Tel: 0481 82 2549

NORTHERN IRELAND
Eglinton Aero Club, Eglinton Airfield, Co Londonderry.
Tel: 0504 810962

St. Angelo Flight Centre, St. Angelo Airport, Enniskillen.
Tel: 0365 22771

Ulster Flying Club, Newtownards Airport. Tel: 0247 813327

Woodgate Air Services Flying School, Belfast (Aldergrove) Airport.
Tel: 08494 22789

Helicopter Training Schools

Aeromega Ltd, Stapleford Aerodrome, Essex RM4 1RL.
Tel: 081 500 3030

Blackpool Air Centre, Blackpool Airport, Lancashire FY4 2QY.
Tel: 0253 41871

Blades Helicopters Ltd, Goodwood Aerodrome, Chichester, Sussex
PO18 0PH. Tel: 0243 779222

Bristow Helicopters, Redhill Aerodrome, Surrey RH1 5JZ.
Tel: 0737 822353

British International Helicopters Ltd, Aberdeen Airport, Dyce, Scotland
AB2 0DT. Tel: 0224 771353

Cabair Helicopters, Elstree Aerodrome, Hertfordshire WD6 3AW and
Redhill Aerodrome, Surrey. Tels: 081 853 4411 and 0737 822166

Cotswold Helicopters, Staverton Airport, Cheltenham, Gloucestershire
GL51 6SR. Tel: 0452 713924

CSE Helicopters, Oxford Airport, Oxford OX5 1RA. Tel: 0865 844239

Delta Helicopters Ltd, Luton Airport, Bedfordshire. Tel: 0582 405250

Dollar Air Services Ltd, Hangar 6, Coventry Airport, Baginton, Warwickshire CV8 3AZ. Tel: 0203 304231

East Midlands Helicopters, Oaklands, Loughborough Road, Costock, Leicestershire LE12 6RQ. Tel: 0509 856464

Exec-H Ltd, Halfpenny Green Airport, West Midlands. Tel: 0388 488 456

FAST Helicopters, Thruxton Aerodrome, Near Andover, Hampshire. Tel: 0264 772508

Heli-Flair Ltd, Goodwood Aerodrome, Near Chichester, West Sussex. Tel: 0243 779222

Heliyorks Flight Training School, Sherburn-in-Elmet Aerodrome, Yorkshire and Newcastle Airport, Tyne & Wear. Tel: 0937 833448

Ipswich Helicopters Ltd, Ipswich Airport, Suffolk. Tel: 0473 725355

Manchester Helicopter Centre, Barton Aerodrome, Eccles, Lancashire. Tel: 061 787 7125

Alan Mann Helicopters Ltd, Fairoaks Airport, Chobham, Surrey GU24 8HU. Tel: 0276 857471

March Helicopters, Sywell Aerodrome, Northamptonshire. Tel: 0604 493137

Northern Helicopters Ltd, Blackpool Airport, Lancashire. Tel: 0253 43082

RM Helicopters Ltd, Leavesden Airport, Near Watford, Hertfordshire WD2 7BY. Tel: 0923 662524

Skyline Helicopters Ltd, Wycombe Air Park, Near Marlow, Buckinghamshire SL7 3DR. Tel: 0494 451111

Sloane Helicopters Ltd, Sywell Aerodrome, Northamptonshire NN6 0BN. Tel: 0604 790595

Southern Air Ltd, The Helicopter Centre, Shoreham Airport, Sussex BN4 5FF. Tel: 0273 461661

Thurston Helicopters (Headcorn) Ltd, Headcorn Aerodrome, Near Lashenden, Kent. Tel: 0622 891158

Trent Air Services Ltd, Cranfield Airport, Cranfield, Bedfordshire MK43 0AL. Tel: 0234 751243

Tyne-Tees Helicopter Centre Ltd, Teesside International Airport, County Durham DL2 1LU. Tel: 0325 333823

Yorkshire Helicopter Centre, Doncaster Airport, Doncaster, South Yorkshire DN4 5HU. Tel: 0302 539189

Professional Flight Training Schools — UK

Air Service Training,
Perth Aerodrome,
Perth,
Scotland PH2 6NP.
Tel: 0738 52311

Bristow Helicopters,
Redhill Aerodrome,
Redhill,
Surrey RH1 1SQ.
Tel: 073 782 2353

British Aerospace Flying College,
Prestwick Airport,
Ayrshire,
Scotland KA9 2RW.
Tel: 0292 79888

G.B. Air Academy,
Goodwood Aerodrome,
Near Chichester,
West Sussex.
Tel: 0243 531516
Fax: 0243 533879

Oxford Air Training School,
Oxford Airport,
Kidlington,
Oxfordshire OX5 1RA.
Tel: 0865 841234

Professional Pilot Study Centre (ground tuition only, no flying)
Bournemouth International Airport,
Christchurch,
Dorset BH23 6DN.
Tel: 0202 579819
Fax: 0202 580150

Trent Flying Training School,
Cranfield Airfield,
Cranfield,
Bedfordshire MK43 0AL.
Tel: 0234 751243

Training Schools abroad offering courses for UK students

Europe

Anglo-Algarve Aviation, Faro International Airport, Faro 8000, Portugal. Tels: UK 0603 738578, Portugal 89.817874

Flight Training International, Cannes-Mandelieu Airport, France. Tel: UK 0959 76828, France 33.93.90.40.19

La Rochelle Flying Centre, La Rochelle-Laleu Airport, France. Tel: UK 0935 841454

United States

Aeronautical Academy of Florida Inc, St Lucie County, Fort Pierce, Florida. UK contact: Melbourne House, Melbourne Street, Brighton BN2 3LH. Tel: UK 0273 674143

American Christian Aviation Institute, Oakland-Pontiac Airport, Pontiac, Michigan 48054. Tel: 313 674 1005

Bolivar Aviation International School of Aeronautics, PO Box 229, Bolivar, Tennessee 38008. Tel: UK 0638 77260

Florida Flight Training Inc, Rockledge Air Park, Florida. UK contact: Flight Training Inc UK Ltd, Southbank House, Black Prince Road, London SE1 7SJ. Tel: UK 071 582 9446

Heliflight Inc, Fort Lauderdale, Florida. UK contact: Flight Training Inc UK Ltd, Southbank House, Black Prince Road, London SE1 7SJ. Tel: UK 071 582 9446

Merritt Island Air Service Inc, 900 Airport Road, Merritt Island, Florida 32952. Tel: USA 407 453 2222

Pelican Airways, North Perry Airport, West Hollywood, Florida 33023. Tels: UK 0233 82264, USA 305 966 9750

Phoenix East Aviation Inc, Daytona Beach, Florida 32014

Sky Breeze Aviation, Lubbock International Airport, Texas. Tels: UK 0895 812330 and 081 893 1221

Sowell Aviation Co Inc, PO Box 1490, Panama City, Florida. Tel: USA 904 785 4325

Treasure Coast Flight Training, Stuart Aviation Centre, Stuart, Florida. Tel: UK 021 454 4353, USA 407 220 0088

Titan Helicopter Academy, Building 90, Easterwood Street, Milville, New Jersey 08332. Tel: USA 609 327 5203

Tyler International (Bay Aviation), Panama City, Florida. UK contact: Meeting House Lane, Baldock, Hertfordshire SG7 5BP. Tel: UK 0462 895800

British airlines, charter and cargo operators

Aberdeen Airways, Viscount House, Aberdeen Airport, Dyce, Scotland AB2 0PA. Tel: 0224 723441

Air Atlantique, Hangar 5, Coventry Airport, Warwickshire CV8 3AZ. Tel: 0203 307566

Air-Bridge Carriers, East Midlands Airport, Castle Donington, Derbyshire DE7 2SA. Tel: 0332 810081

Air Europe, The Galleria, Station Road, Crawley, West Sussex RH10 1HY. Tel: 0293 562626

Air Europe Express, Europe House, Manor Royal, West Sussex RH10 2QD. Tel: 0293 562626

Air Excel, Kensal House, 1–4 President Way, Luton International Airport, Bedfordshire LU2 9LU. Tel: 0582 480911

Air Foyle, Halcyon House, Luton Airport, Bedfordshire LU2 9LU. Tel: 0582 412792

Air UK, Stansted House, London-Stansted Airport, Essex CM24 8QT. Tel: 0279 755950

Air UK Leisure, Airways House, London-Stansted Airport, Essex CM24 8RY. Tel: 0279 755223

Air 2000, Oakdale, Broadfield Park, Crawley, West Sussex RH11 9RT. Tel: 0293 518966

Aurigny Air Services, The Airport, Alderney, Channel Islands. Tel: 0481 822886

Birmingham European Airways, Hangar 1, Birmingham International Airport, Birmingham B26 3QB. Tel: 021 782 0521

Bond Air Services, Aberdeen Airport, Dyce, Aberdeen AB2 0DU. Tel: 0224 725505

Bristow Helicopters, Redhill Aerodrome, Redhill, Surrey RH1 5JZ. Tel: 073 782 2353

Britannia Airways, Luton Airport, Bedfordshire LU2 9ND. Tel: 0582 424155

British Air Ferries, Viscount House, Southend Airport, Southend-on-Sea, Essex SS2 6YL. Tel: 0702 354435

British Airways, Speedbird House, London-Heathrow Airport, Middlesex TW6 2JA. Tel: 081 759 5511

British International Helicopters, Hollow Way, Cowley, Oxford OX4 2PH. Tel: 0865 747066

British Midland Airways, Donington Hall, Castle Donington, Derbyshire DE7 2SB. Tel: 0332 810741

Brymon Airways, Plymouth City Airport, Crownhill, Plymouth, Devon PL6 8TP. Tel: 0752 705151

Caledonian Airways, Airtours House, Gatwick Airport, West Sussex RH6 0LF. Tel: 0293 36321

Channel Express (Air Services), Bournemouth International Airport, Christchurch, Dorset BH23 6DL. Tel: 0202 570701

Dan-Air Services, New City Court, 20 St Thomas Street, London SE1 9RJ. Tel: 071 378 6464

DHL Air, East Midlands Airport, Castle Donington, Derby DE7 2SB. Tel: 0332 850666

Euroair, Gatwick House, Peeks Lane, Horley, Surrey RH6 9SU. Tel: 0293 820732

Guernsey Airlines, Guernsey Airport, La Villiaze, Guernsey, Channel Islands. Tel: 0481 35727

Heavylift Cargo Airlines, London-Stansted Airport, Stansted, Essex CM24 8QP. Tel: 0279 680611

Instone Air Line, Unit 13, Church Road, Lowfield Heath, Crawley, West Sussex RH11 0PQ. Tel: 0293 511271

Inter European Airways, 3 Bute Place, Cardiff, Wales CF1 6AL. Tel: 0222 465533

Jersey European Airways, Terminal Building, Exeter Airport, Clyst Honiton, Devon EX5 2BD. Tel: 0392 66669

Loganair, St Andrews Drive, Glasgow Airport, Paisley, Scotland PA3 2TG. Tel: 041 889 1311

London City Airways, London City Airport, London E16 2QQ. Tel: 071 474 2230

Manx Airlines, Ronaldsway Airport, Ballasalla, Isle of Man. Tel: 0624 824111

Monarch Airlines, Luton International Airport, Bedfordshire LU2 9NU. Tel: 0582 424211

Scottish European Airways, Admin Block B, St Andrews Drive, Glasgow Airport, Paisley, Scotland PA3 2SG. Tel: 041 887 7700

Suckling Airways, Ipswich Airport, Suffolk IP3 9QF. Tel: 0473 718346

TEA UK, Old Terminal Building, Birmingham International Airport, Birmingham B26 3QN. Tel: 021 782 2323

TNT, Archway House, 114–116 St Leonards Road, Windsor, Berkshire SL4 3DG. Tel: 0753 842168

Tradewinds Airways, Building 73, London-Stansted Airport, Essex CM24 8QW. 0279 816404

Virgin Atlantic Airways, Ashdown House, High Street, Crawley, West Sussex RH10 1DQ. Tel: 0293 562345

Useful addresses — Private Pilots

Aircraft Owners and Pilots
Association,
50A Cambridge Street,
London SW1V 4QQ.
Tel: 071 834 5631

Air Education & Recreation
Organisation
South West Area Education
Office,
14A/B North Street,
Guildford,
Surrey GU1 4AF.
Tel: 0483 572881

Air League Educational Trust,
Grey Tiles,
Kingston Hill,
Kingston-uon-Thames,
Surrey KT2 7LW.
Tel: 081 546 9325

Amy Johnson Memorial Trust,
12 Church Lane,
Merton Park,
London SW19 3PD.
Tel: 081 540 1797

British Aerobatic Association,
'Channings',
Littleheath Road,
Fontwell,
Arundel,
Sussex BN18 0SR.
Tel: 0243 543263

British Gliding Association,
Kimberley House,
Vaughan Way,
Leicester LE1 4SE.
Tel: 0533 531051

British Microlight Aircraft
Assocation,
The Bullring,
Deddington,
Oxfordshire OX5 4TT.
Tel: 0869 38888

British Precision Pilots
Association,
2 Park Avenue,
Harpenden,
Hertfordshire AL5 2EA.
Tel: 05827 65072

British Women Pilots Association,
Rochester Airport,
Chatham,
Kent ME5 9SD.
Tel: 0634 816340

Civil Aviation Authority,
Flight Crew Licensing (Private
Pilots)
Aviation House,
South Area,
Gatwick Airport,
West Sussex RH6 0YR.
Tel: 0293 567171 Exts. 3580/1

Civil Aviation Authority Medical
Branch,
Aviation House,
South Area,
Gatwick Airport,
West Sussex RH6 0YR.
Tel: 0293 567171 Ext. 3685

Formula Air Racing Association,
86 Tresillian Road,
Brockley,
London SE4 1YD

Girls Venture Corps,
Redhill Aerodrome,
Kings Mill Lane,
South Nutfield,
Redhill,
Surrey RH1 5JY.
Tel: 0737 823345

Helicopter Club of Great Britain,
Ryelands House,
Aynho,
Banbury,
Oxfordshire OX17 3AT.
Tel: 0869 810646

International Air Tattoo Flying
Scholarships for the Disabled,
IAT Building 1108,
RAF Fairford,
Gloucestershire GL7 4DL.
Tel: 0285 713300

Popular Flying Association,
Terminal Building,
Shoreham Airport,
Sussex BN4 5FF.
Tel: 0273 461616

Royal Aero Club,
Kimberley House,
Vaughan Way,
Leicester LE1 4SG.
Tel: 0533 531051

Useful addresses — Commercial and Airline Pilots

Air Training Association,
125 London Road,
High Wycombe,
Buckinghamshire HP11 1BT.
Tel: 0494 445262

British Airline Pilots Association,
81 New Road,
Harlington,
Hayes,
Middlesex UB3 5BG
Tel: 081 759 9331

British Helicopter Advisory Board,
Building C2,
West Entrance,
Fairoaks Airport,
Chobham,
Surrey GU24 8HC.
Tel: 0990 56100

Business Aircraft Users
Association,
PO Box 29,
Wallingford,
Oxfordshire OX10 0AG.
Tel: 0941 37903

Civil Aviation Authority,
Professional Flight Crew
Licensing,
Aviation House,
South Area,
Gatwick Airport,
West Sussex RH6 0YR.
Tel: 0293 567171 Exts. 3565/6

Civil Aviation Authority Medical
Department,
Aviation House,
South Area,
Gatwick Airport,
West Sussex RH6 0YR.
Tel: 0293 567171 Ext. 3685

General Aviation Manufacturers &
Traders Association,
26 High Street,
Brill,
Aylesbury,
Buckinghamshire HP18 9ST.
Tel: 0844 238389

Guild of Air Pilots & Air
Navigators,
291 Gray's Inn Road,
London WC1X 8QF.
Tel: 071 837 3323

Student Pilot's Association,
30 Tisbury Road,
Hove,
East Sussex BN3 3BA.
Tel: 0273 204080

Useful addresses: Military Pilots

Royal Air Force Officer Careers,
London Road,
Stanmore,
Middlesex HA7 4PZ.

Royal Air Force Officer and
Aircrew Selection Centre,
RAF Biggin Hill,
Westerham,
Kent.

RAF University Liaison Offices:
London and S.E. England
ULO, RAF Officer Careers,
Government Buildings,
London Road,
Stanmore,
Middlesex HA7 4PZ.
Tel: 081 958 6377 ext. 3151

S. Wales and S.W. England
ULO, RAF Lyneham
Chippenham,
Wiltshire SN15 4PZ.
Tel: 0249 890987/890381 Ext. 228

N. Wales, W. Midlands and
N. W. England
ULO, RAF Cosford,
Wolverhampton,
West Midlands WV7 3EX.
Tels: 090722 2393 Ext. 367
or 090722 4172/4174

E. Midlands and Yorkshire
ULO, RAF Newton,
Nottinghamshire NG13 8HL.
Tels: 0949 20771 Ext. 376
or 0949 20020

Scotland, N. Ireland and
N.E. England
ULO, RAF Turnhouse,
Edinburgh EH12 0AQ.
Tels: 031 339 2312
or 031 339 5393 Ext. 212

Officer Commanding,
University Air Squadrons,
RAF College Cranwell,
Sleaford,
Lincolnshire NG34 8HB.
Tel: 0400 61201

Director of Recruiting,
RAF Careers Information Centre,
302 Regent Street,
London W1.

Air Cadets & Air Training Corps,
Headquarters Air Cadets,
RAF Newton,
Nottinghamshire NG13 8HR.
Tel: 0949 20771

RAF Careers Information Offices are located in the following towns:

Aberdeen	Exeter	Oldham
Aldergrove	Glasgow	Oxford
Ayr	Gloucester	Peterborough
Bangor	Grimsby	Plymouth
Bedford	Guildford	Portsmouth
Birmingham	Hamilton	Preston
Blackburn	Huddersfield	Reading
Blackheath	Hull	St. Helens
Blackpool	Ilford	Sheffield
Bournemouth	Inverness	Shrewsbury
Bradford	Ipswich	Southampton
Brighton	Leeds	Southend
Bristol	Leicester	Stockport
Cambridge	Lincoln	Stoke-on-Trent
Canterbury	Liverpool	Sunderland
Cardiff	London	Swansea
Carlisle	Luton	Swindon
Chatham	Manchester	Taunton
Coventry	Middlesbrough	Truro
Darlington	Newcastle	Watford
Derby	Newport	Wolverhampton
Doncaster	Norbury	Wrexham
Dundee	Norwich	York
Edinburgh	Nottingham	

Royal Navy,
Officer Entry Section,
Royal Naval Careers Service,
Old Admiralty Building,
Spring Gardens,
London SW1A 2BE.
Tel: 071 218 7011.

RO2 Army Air Corps Regimental
Affairs, (Officer entry)
Headquarters,
Director Army Air Corps,
Middle Wallop,
Stockbridge,
Hants SO20 8DY.

Recruiting Liaison Officer,
(NCOs)
Headquarters,
Director Army Air Corps,
Middle Wallop,
Stockbridge, Hants SO20 8DY.
Tel: 0264 62121. Ext. 216

Suppliers of Pilot Equipment and Publications

Aero Shopping,
50A Cambridge Street,
London SW1V 4QQ
Tel: 071 834 9307

Airplan Flight Equipment,
Building 523A Southside,
Manchester International Airport,
Wilmslow,
Cheshire SK9 4LL.
Tel: 061 499 0023/4
Fax: 061 499 0298

Airtour International,
Elstree Aerodrome,
Borehamwood,
Hertfordshire.
Tel: 081 953 4870 and 6064

Beaumont Aviation Literature,
656 Holloway Road,
London N19 3PD.
Tel: 071 272 3630

Civil Aviation Authority
Publications Department,
Greville House,
37 Gratton Road,
Cheltenham,
Gloucestershire GL50 2BN.
Tel: 0242 235151
Fax: 0242 584139

CAA publications also available to
personal callers only from
CAA Library,
45–59 Kingsway,
London WC2B 6TE.
Tel: 071 379 7311
Fax: 071 240 1153

Harry Mendelssohn Discount
Sales,
34 Buckstone Road,
Edinburgh EH10 6UA.
Tel: 031 445 4444
Fax: 031 445 4454

Midland Counties Publications,
24 The Hollow,
Earl Shilton,
Leicester LE9 7NA.
Tel: 0455 847091
Fax: 0455 841805

Motor Books,
33 St Martin's Court,
London WC2N 4AL.
Tel: 071 836 5376

Transair Pilot Shop,
West Entrance,
Fairoaks Airport,
Chobham,
Surrey GU24 8HX.
Tel: 0276 858533

Glossary

AAC	Army Air Corps
ADF	Automatic Direction Finder
AFI	Assistant Flying Instructor
AH	Artificial Horizon
AIC	Aeronautical Information Circular
AIS	Aeronautical Information Service
ANO	Air Navigation Order
AOC	Air Operators Certificate
AOPA	Aircraft Owners and Pilots' Association
ASI	Airspeed Indicator
ATC	Air Traffic Controller (or Air Training Corps)
ATCO	Air Traffic Control Officer
ATPL	Air Transport Pilot's Licence
ATZ	Aerodrome Traffic Zone
BA	British Airways
BAe	British Aerospace
BALPA	British Airline Pilots' Association
BCPL	Basic Commercial Pilot's Licence
BHAB	British Helicopter Advisory Board
CAA	Civil Aviation Authority
CAP	Civil Air Publication
CCF	Combined Cadet Force
CFI	Chief Flying Instructor
CFS	(RAF) Central Flying School
CofA	Certificate of Airworthiness
CofG	Centre of Gravity (or CG)
CPL	Commercial Pilot's Licence
DF	Direction Finding
DG	Directional Gyro
DI	Direction Indicator (or Daily Inspection)
DME	Distance Measuring Equipment
EFIS	Electronic Flight Information System
EFTS	Elementary Flying Training School (RAF)
FAA	Federal Aviation Administration (USA) or Fleet Air Arm
FIR	Flight Information Region
FIS	Flight Information Service
FTS	Flying Training School
GAMTA	General Aviation Manufacturers & Traders Association
GFT	General Flying Test
IAS	Indicated Airspeed
IF	Instrument Flying
IFR	Instrument Flight Rules
ILS	Instrument Landing System

IMC	Instrument Meteorological Conditions
INS	Inertial Navigation System
IR	Instrument Rating
MATZ	Military Aerodrome Traffic Zone
NATS	National Air Traffic Services
NDB	Non-Directional Beacon
NFT	Navigation Flight Test
NOTAM	Notices to Airmen
OASC	Officer and Aircrew Selection Centre
OATS	Oxford Air Training School
OCU	(RAF) Operational Conversion Unit
PFA	Popular Flying Association
PPL	Private Pilot's Licence
QFE	Atmospheric Pressure at aerodrome elevation
QFI	Qualified Flying Instructor
QNH	Atmospheric Pressure at sea level
RAF	Royal Air Force
RAFVR	Royal Air Force Volunteer Reserve
RN	Royal Navy
RT	Radiotelephony
SATCO	Senior Air Traffic Control Officer
SPL	Student Pilot's Licence
STOVL	Short Take-off/Vertical Landing
TAS	True Airspeed
TMA	Terminal Control Area (of an aerodrome)
TWU	(RAF) Tactical Weapons Unit
UAS	University Air Squadron
UHF	Ultra High Frequency
VFR	Visual Flight Rules
VGS	Volunteer Gliding School
VHF	Very High Frequency
VMC	Visual Meteorological Conditions
VOR	VHF Omni-range
VSI	Vertical Speed Indicator
V/STOL	Vertical/Short Take-Off and Landing
Zulu	Greenwich Mean Time